Thanks
Pastor for
being dedicated to
youth
4-18-07   E. Hoffman

EARL HOFFMEISTER

*Knox County Schools
Superintendent
1976 - 1992*

by Benna F. J. van Vuuren

TENNESSEE VALLEY
Publishing
2007

Copyright © 2007

All rights reserved. No part of this book may be reproduced in any form or by any electronic or mechanical means including information storage and retrieval systems without permission in writing from the publisher, except by a reviewer, who may quote brief passages in a review.

Library of Congress Control Number: 2006938702

Published by:
    Tennessee Valley Publishing
    PO Box 52527
    Knoxville, Tennessee 37950-2527

Printed and bound in the United States of America.

ISBN 978-1-932604-42-9

About the Author

Benna F. J. van Vuuren

The author's professional career has spanned more than 50 years. Ms. van Vuuren was educated in the Knoxville City Schools and completed her education at the University of Tennessee where she received a Bachelor of Arts Degree with a teaching certificate in 1955. She completed her Master of Science Degree in Administration and Supervision with a minor in English in 1964. Later she completed a year's work at the University of South Africa in the Masters Program in Business Leadership, 45 hours in the doctoral program in Administration and Supervision at the University of Tennessee.

Ms. van Vuuren has served as a teacher, elementary principal, elementary supervisor in Knox County Schools. She worked for both Miss Doyle and Mr. Hoffmeister. She was Principal of Amherst School and Asbury School. As a Central Office Supervisor she was a member of both Miss Doyle's and Mr. Hofmeister's staff. Ms. van Vuuren worked as Title I Consultant establishing Parent Advisory Council. Also, as Director of the Knox County Reading is Fundamental Program, she introduced the program and established it system wide.

In 1981, she founded the American International School in Johannesburg in South Africa and served as its first superintendent. Returning to the states, Ms. van Vuuren worked as a State Department Consultant on a special program – Improving Proficiency Test Scores in Targeted Schools in East Tennessee.

For the past seven years, she has operated the VAN VUUREN ACADEMY, a small private school in Union County. She is currently heavily involved in establishing the Knox County Museum of Educational History at the Historic Knoxville High School.

JoAnne and Earl Hoffmeister.   Jean and Gene Payne.

Dedication

This book is dedicated to Earl Hoffmeister, his lovely wife JoAnne and all the wonderful folks in the Knox County School System who supported him and helped make Knox County School an outstanding system – especially the ones who also made it fun.

And to Jean Payne and her husband, without whom it would never have happened.

A special thanks, also, to the most patient typist ever – Carolyn Hall – who made endless corrections.

How This Biography Came To Be Written

Beginning in the Spring of 2005, I had become aware of the lack of a history of Knox County Schools and its many colorful educators especially the two superintendents with whom I had worked. There had been two dissertations on Miss Doyle and one biography; neither of these really captured the Mildred E. Doyle that I had enjoyed and admired.

Years before her death, I had talked to her about writing her autobiography or even working with someone else to write one. She admitted that she had thought about it; she had even come up with a title *Broaden Me Out, Mildred* based on a request frequently made by a woman who faithfully attended the School Board Meetings. I guess that I felt and still do feel that nothing has been written that really "broadened" out Miss Doyle. I wonder if anything really could without her input.

It suddenly occurred to me that the same thing was going to happen to Earl Hoffmeister. I double checked to see if any dissertation had been written on him or any biography. Finding that nothing had been written, I phoned him and told him about my dissatisfaction with the biographies of Miss Doyle; I suggested that he had better have his biography written while he was still living and could defend himself.

I even warned him (tongue in cheek) that if he didn't get it written, the only account would be by some graduate student who would write a dissertation about him and swear that he could neither read nor write or find his way out of a building – since he had been a coach. I received a typical Hoffmeister reply – "Benna, they probably can document all three." But he did think about it and asked me to help him write it.

I determined at the beginning that this biography would not be a critical analysis of Mr. Hoffmeister or his tenure as

Superintendent. I would not attempt to include every detail of his sixteen years in office. Instead, it would focus on Earl's uniqueness and be a celebration of his life. I would make no apology for writing it from my own personal point of view.

    I have included an appendix at the end to show what a complex organization Earl found when he became Superintendent in 1976 and how few changes he made in Central Office Staff members. Also, these lists and the photographs included in the book bring back memories of a wonderful era in Knox County Schools.

List of Photographs

Some photographs of marginal quality were included in this book, because they were the best that could be obtained and the individuals are important to Mr. Hoffmeister's story.

1. Earl, mother Thelma, brother H.L. and father, Hoff . . . 4
2. Young High School Memories–Coach Cecil Stone
    & Earl Hoffmeister, outstanding atheletse 10
3. Earl in Army uniform 13
4. Principal Homer Sharp 15
5. W. W. Morris, Superintendent of Powell High 16
6. Earl McCall, Principal of Powell High 16
7. Dan Boring, Principal of Central High 16
8. Dan Hoffmeister 17
9. David and wife Jenny 18
10. Jason, son of David, with bride Michelle 18
11. Deborah, husband Gerald Johnson and son Will 19
12. Earl and brother H.L. in his Navy Uniform 20
13. Faye Cox - Secretary for Miss Doyle and
    Mr. Hoffmeister 34
14 Beecher Clapp 37
15. Earl and his Kitchen Cabinet: Dr. Fred Bedelle,
    Tommy Schumpert, Earl, Dr. Richard Yoakley,
    Jim Robinson and Beecher Clapp 38
16. Ruth Clapp, Kindergarten Supervisor for both
    Knox County and Knoxville City. 38
17. Dr. Anne Meek 38
18. Lanoka Rhodes 39
19. Mary Jo Husk 39
20. Sue Boyer 39
21. Willa Silvey 39
22. Elizabeth Wells, Earl's secretary 39
23. Bobb Goff, Supervisor of Middle School Education . . 40

24.	Dr. William Phifer, Supervisor of Secondary Education	40
25.	Virginia Underwood, Reading Superisor	41
26.	Charlene De Ridder, Mathematics Supervisor	41
27.	Sarah Simpson, Language Arts Supervisor	41
28.	Jane Humble Doyle, Social Studies Supervisor	42
29.	Bob Chambers, Science Supervisor	42
30.	VaLera Lewis, Art Supervisor	43
31.	J. B. Lyle, Music Supervisor	44
32.	Carolyn Sullivan, Psys Ed., Driver Ed. and Health Supervisor	44
33.	Benna van Vuuren, Title I and RIF Supervisor	45
34.	Dr. Sam Bratton, Research and Evaluation Supervisor	45
35.	Dr. J. B. Bolin, Adult Education Supervisor	46
36.	Bill Orr, Transportation Supervisor	46
37.	Dr. Joseph Chandler, Personnel Supervisor	46
38.	Bill Clabo and Earl Hoffmeister	62
39.	Bill Padgett and wife	67
40.	Margaret Clabo Pattison and JoAnne Hoffmeister	67
41.	John R. McCloud and Mary Kerr	68
42.	John Dobbs and Jack Cooper	68
43.	Reed, Mary and Margaret Garrison; Paul Monger; Jean Payne; and JoAnne and Earl Hoffmeister	68
44.	Tommy Schumpert	73
45.	Preacher Mull and wife, Elizabeth	74
46.	Earl Hoffmeister, football player	75
47.	Earl and Peggy Dison, Homebound Student	78
48.	Sarah Simpson and Larry Bates, Homebound Student	79
49.	Earl Hoffmeister, President Ronald Reagan and Jim Bellamy, Principal of Farragut	83
50.	Earl Hoffmeister, President George H. Bush and	

50. Rex Stooksbury 84
51. Earl in Taiwan 86
52. Earl on Safari 87

Table of Contents

Introduction xii
Chapter 1
    The Background of Earl Hoffmeister 1
Chapter 2
    Young High School 11
Chapter 3
    The Election of 1976 21
Chapter 4
    The Beginning of a New Era 33
Chapter 5
    Politician and Manager 57
Chapter 6
    Accomplishments and Honors 75
Chapter 7
    Conclusions 91
References/Acknowledgments 95
Appendix I 96

Introduction

This is more than a biography of Earl Hoffmeister; it is a tribute to the "best person who could have defeated Miss Doyle" and served as Superintendent of Knox County Schools after a 30 year reign by Miss Doyle.

The author of this biography comes from a generation of folks who would never have referred to either of these superintendents by their first names, and who admired both. I idolized Miss Doyle: I worked for her as a teacher, principal and supervisor. I sometimes went meekly on missions that were someone else's territory because she had snagged me as I went by her always open door; I sometimes stood up to her and refused – taking a good verbal shellacking before she cooled down. Knowing Miss Doyle, working for her and loving her was one of the biggest highlights of my life. I never met Mr. Hoffmeister until he walked into the Central Office after defeating Miss Doyle.

How did it happen? Why did Miss Doyle lose an election to a man with little, if any, administrative or system-wide experience, and why was Mr. Hoffmeister the perfect person to succeed her?

This is the author's answer to both questions, and I am sure that everyone involved at the time had his or her own answer – but this is mine. To begin with, Miss Doyle had not intended to run again. She had groomed Beecher Clapp to succeed her. But she could not sell the idea to the "old boys" in the Republican Party who did not believe that Mr. Clapp could be elected. The "powers that be" insisted that Miss Doyle run again. As she stated once to me, she doubted that she could be elected again because she hadn't planned to run, so she had made a lot of people mad. But I always thought the final straw was the Gold Cadillac.

Expecting Miss Doyle to retire, the teachers in Knox County Schools and other personnel had collected money to buy Miss Doyle a Cadillac as her retirement present; this did not go down well when she decided to run again. The Cadillac was presented to Miss Doyle in a packed gym at Doyle High School December 1, 1975. Billy K. Nicely ended the program honoring Miss Doyle and her 30 years of service by stating that the Cadillac could be Miss Doyle's birthday present, (Miss Doyle would be 71 later on in December) and there was no reason she could not drive it for the next four years as superintendent. The cat was out of the bag.

From January until August, Knox County Schools went on as usual. Whatever Beecher Clapp thought or felt everyone did their best to garner support for Miss Doyle. It did not dawn on most of us that she could possibly not be elected. I had never heard of Mr. Hoffmeister and was surprised when he announced his intention to run. I read about his difficulties getting a superintendent's endorsement and the expected disparaging remarks about him just being a coach. In spite of the lack of enthusiasm about Miss Doyle's candidacy, no one expected her to lose.

But election night arrived and we were all gathered to hear the returns come in – and come in they did – and the unbelievable happened. Miss Doyle lost the election. It was like a death in the family! And the days that followed were worse. Miss Doyle could not rise to the occasion and begin to hand over to Mr. Hoffmeister. Instead she spent the last days of her 30 year term in office trying to come up with some way of still controlling Knox County Schools.

In meetings, she assured us we would be all right, that the budget was in place and everything would go on as usual. I was so disappointed – she was my idol – I expected so much more. But it was obvious that she thought she could still run things through her staff. But she was wrong, and if she had thought about it she would have known it was wrong. By and large her staff was "what she had raised us to be," and we would work for Knox County Schools first – and then for Mr. Hoffmeister.

At the presentation ceremony, Beecher Clapp had worn a light colored suit and carried on with such grace that it moved me to tears as I thought what a gallant man he was, but he would never be our "white knight." The first time I saw Mr. Hoffmeister, he too had on a white suit; he walked hesitantly into the Central Office. No one came out to greet him. But as I was walking across the open area, I went over and greeted him. I was struck by his humility and friendliness and I suddenly thought,"Maybe this is our white knight."

Mr. Hoffmeister won me over by his humility; he never pretended to know anything he did not know. He was never anything but respectful toward Miss Doyle, and he never called her by her first name. He referred to the Central Office staff as the "best in the state," and let them get on with running the school system. But he was no fool and there was no weakness in him. He instinctively knew whom to trust and whom not to trust. The person that he chose to depend most on was Beecher Clapp, and I realized Mr. Hoffmeister might not be the same type of leader as Miss Doyle, but he was a leader – and he could be trusted with the Knox County Schools.

Chapter 1
The Background of Earl Hoffmeister

It would be a disservice to Mr. Hoffmeister to try to reduce him and his life to a standard formal biography. Therefore, along with the usual birth, education, work experiences, this biography is going to be based in part on Mr. Hoffmeister's often humorous, folksy remembrances and interpretation of his life.

Before I could get started asking him about his family background, he interrupted me to tell me that I needed to know he was the ugliest baby anyone had ever seen, and that his mother had cried for three weeks because he was a boy. Of course, if he had been a girl and looked like that, she would have cried longer. He said there was only one baby picture made of him and that one was made of him and the family dog. People who saw it always hesitated and then commented on the nice looking dog.

But then Mr. Hoffmeister spoke with a great deal of pride about being able to trace his ancestry back to Germany to the days of Charlemagne. According to the research that James T. Hoffmeister compiled in 1922, the Hoffmeister name goes back to an ancestor who held that office under Charlemagne: it was equivalent to the English Court Master. It was a position of great importance and dignity. The ancestor held that position under Charlemagne from 786 to 814 A.D. and the title followed him and his descendants afterward as a surname. James T. Hoffmeister stated the courts of Germany and Austria both had their official Hoffmeisters up until World War I.

Earl is the seventh generation of Hoffmeisters who came to the United States from Germany. The first one was Gottlieb Hoffmeister who was born in the vicinity of Frankfort around 1767. He changed his name to Godlove after he and his wife

Sarah Lauderback came to America and settled in Shennadoah County, Virginia. His nine children were all born in Virginia before the family moved to Hawkins County, Tennessee where he bought land in 1811.

His oldest son, Joseph, married Elizabeth Weitzel and fought with General Andrew Jackson during the War of 1812. He took part in the Battle of Horseshoe Bend where the Creek nation was virtually destroyed. Joseph was commissioned as a Captain; he later served as a Justice of the Peace, an Entry Taker for Public Lands and as an Elder in the Presbyterian Church.

One of his 13 children was Samuel Louderback Hoffmeister (April 12, 1813 - July 19, 1882) who married Elizabeth Counts. They moved to Morristown where he was involved in the building of the mill there. He was a member of the Methodist Church and a Master Mason. One of his sons, Joseph Martin Hoffmeister (October 16, 1937 - March 8, 1917) was Earl's great-grandfather. He married Mary E. Sehorn and they moved to the Knoxville area. Joseph served in the 60th Tennessee Regiment of the Confederate Army.

Earl's grandfather was James A. Hoffmeister (October, 1876 - September 25, 1921). He married Lena May Evans and lived at Powell Station, Tennessee right outside Knoxville. He and his wife had nine children. Earl's father, Hollis, was the oldest. He had seven sisters and a brother, Jim, who was the youngest. Earl likes to tell of two of the girls – Pauline and Aline – who were twins and were so small a teacup would fit over the heads. Their parents made an "incubator" using the oven of the cook stove to keep them at a constant temperature, and amazingly they survived. Jim eventually became a doctor.

Earl enjoys telling of the diversity of his family background. The Hoffmeisters chose many different careers. Some were farmers; several were soldiers, and a few were doctors and lawyers. One – Weitzel Hoffmeister – went off to Texas and got himself written up as an Indian fighter in a book by Betty Zane.

Hoffmeister's father, Hollis – who was always called Hoff, was born October 15, 1899. Hoff's father, James A. Hoffmeister, died not long after the birth of the youngest child, Jim, was born. This left his mother with nine children. Hollis was the oldest and the responsibility fell on him. Besides working on the farm, Hoff had also helped his father in a livery stable. Later Hoff went to Nashville and worked in a plant. This was during the great flu epidemic, and he often recounted driving a truck that picked up bodies, stacking them like cards and taking them to a makeshift mortuary.

Hoffmeister's father, like many of his generation, only finished the sixth grade, but he was a very intelligent man and could add a column of figures with a pencil faster than most people could add them with a calculator. He also excelled in auto mechanics and was known as a truck and car genius. People would come from miles around for him to diagnose what was wrong with their engines. Later when he had his own bus line, he always did his own mechanical work. From an early age, Earl was put to work washing parts and learning to be a mechanic himself.

Mr. Hoffmeister likes to recount his father had him tear down the same engine five times until he finally gave up getting it right. His dad sent him to fetch a wrench and a hammer, crawled underneath, loosened one bolt and gave it a tap or two with the hammer. The engine ran like a sewing machine. Earl questioned as to why he had him tear it down five times which he could have fixed at that point. His father's reply said it all, "Because you were getting better each time." Earl said that his dad was always careful to let you work out your own problems, but he was always there to help you.

EARL HOFFMEISTER KNOX COUNTY SCHOOLS SUPERINTENDENT

One of Hoffmeister's favorite stories about his father's diagnostic ability concerns five of the top mechanics in the area bringing him a 1936 Chevrolet that was making a strange noise. One of the men was the head of the Tennessee Coach Company that serviced Greyhound buses; and two of them worked at R.T. Clapp. They told him they had a bet among themselves as to what was causing the noise, and they wanted him to settle it. Earl raised the hood of the car, revved the engine and listened carefully. He then went into his shop and returned with a wire coat hanger which he had straightened. Using the coat hanger, he pulled out a piece of cardboard from under the radiator. The cardboard fluttered every time the motor was revved. The five men got back into the car and drove off without saying a word mortified by the whole incident. Hoff just laughed.

Earl, his mother Thelma, his brother H.L. and his father Hoff.

Hoff owned a Willis Agency which was the forerunner of the Jeep Agency. From the time Earl was 16 or so, his father had him working on cars. One of Earl's tasks was to replace clutches. His father had him working in a back room because the customers would not have wanted a boy of that age working on their cars. Earl earned $3.00 of the $7.50 that his dad charged for replacing the clutch.

Another favorite story of Earl's concerning his dad is an incident that happened during World War II. His dad was driving a bus from Knoxville to Sevierville up Chapman Highway. The busses were always overcrowded as the few people who owned cars couldn't get enough gas to drive back and forth because gas was rationed. One bitter, cold night his dad stopped at the end of Henley Street Bridge where a man was waiting for the bus. Hoff opened the door and told him he would have to catch the bus in the rear. What Hoff meant was that the man would have to catch the bus that was following him. The man, unbeknownst to the driver, went to the rear of the bus, climbed up the ladder, and clung to the rails of the luggage rack. When the bus stopped near the gap in the mountain to let some passengers off, the man, frozen blue, suddenly appeared at the door and told the startled driver that since he didn't have room for him except on the top, he'd just walk, and took off walking into the night.

Another time a woman was riding the bus that Hoff was driving, and she had a baby that was squalling. She was attempting to quiet the baby by breast feeding, but the baby continued to squall at the top of its' lungs. Finally in exasperation, the woman announced so that everyone could hear, "If you don't take it, I'll give it to the bus driver." Hoff was kidded about that until he died.

Hoffmeister also likes to tell stories about his family spending six months a year on a place they owned near the Little Tennessee River in what is now the Smoky Mountains National Park. This was before Earl and his brother were old enough to go to school. Hoffmeister was born December 9, 1926 in Maryville, Tennessee, and he vividly remembers the CCC Camp that was nearby. The CCC's were the Civilian Conservation Corps that was set up as part of the New Deal. Mr. Hoffmeister likes to point out that the CCC trained a lot of our soldiers for World War II. (In fact, more than two million young men served in the CCC before Congress abolished it in 1942). But in the early and mid 1930's, the corps provided employment and training for young men; they drilled one half of the day and spent the rest of the time planting trees, restoring farmlands, building dams and fighting forest fires.

There was a CCC Camp near where the Hoffmeisters lived, and on a Saturday night boxing contests were held at the camp. The final boxing event was often between Earl and his brother who were four or five years old. They would really slug it out much to the amusement of everyone. Earl says it always ended in a draw. He always completes the story this way.

"Back then, they put salt peter in the water to take the edge off the sex drive of those young boys. It must have been powerful stuff for here it is 70 years later, and the stuff is just now beginning to kick in on me."

Hoffmeister recalls what a beautiful place it was to live. It was right on the river, and there was a big rock where his father taught lots of people to swim. His method was to toss them off the rock and watch them dog paddle to the land; he only had to pull one person out of the water. Everyone else swam after they had been thrown off the rock and dog paddled to the bank.

Earl also said his dad was quite a marksman with a rifle and a pistol. He cited one incident where his dad shot off the head of a snake as it crawled out from under a rock on which his aunt was sitting. He didn't recount what the effect was on the aunt.

Mr. Hoffmeister speaks lovingly of his mother, Thelma Fowler Hoffmeister. His favorite serious story about her concerns the pies she baked for numerous young men who were away from home during World War II. Earl said she would go all around the neighborhood begging for sugar which was rationed, to bake those pies, and then she would box them up and <u>mail</u> them to various young men. One of them — a pecan pie — was sent to John Clabo who went to high school and played football with the Hoffmeister boys. John's pie was mailed to California, but he had shipped out before it arrived. It followed him through Hawaii and finally caught up with him months later "somewhere in the Pacific." John later recounted that when he opened the package, the pie was encased in green mold. When people sympathized with his loss, John grinned and told them he scrapped off the mold and ate the whole thing – best pecan pie he ever ate. Later John's brother Bill would run against Earl in the "polite campaign of 1980."

By the time Earl was ready to enter first grade, the family was living in Knoxville in the Lincoln Park School zone. He remembers his first grade teacher tied him in his seat and taped his mouth shut, and he also recounts how he failed first grade. His brother got diphtheria that year and the resulting quarantine caused them to miss a good part of the school year. He mentioned how this experience served him well as Superintendent of Schools. He could relate this personal experience to parents who were concerned about their children being held back.

Earl remembers his days at Lincoln Park fondly, recalling the principal was a Miss Kennedy. A Miss Hammer taught music and handwriting. One teacher who left a lasting impression was a Miss Tobe who taught social studies. Miss Tobe was a Jewish lady who had traveled to the Holy Land and many parts of Europe visiting places her students could only dream of.

By the time Earl was ready for sixth grade, his family had moved to South Knox County where he was to attend

White Elementary School for the next three years. White Elementary was very different from Lincoln Park; it only had three rooms. Earl was in a class that contained sixth, seventh and eighth grades. It was taught by one teacher who was also the principal.

His first teacher at White Elementary was a man named Mr. Fritz who retired at the end of Earl's first year. Earl estimates that every boy got paddled at least once a week. They must have driven Mr. Fritz to distraction. Lunch was supposed to be over when Mr. Fritz rang the bell, but often the bell wouldn't ring because the boys had tied a knot in the bell rope. Mr. Fritz would be frustrated trying to round them up for afternoon classes. So Mr. Fritz retired.

In the fall of Earl's seventh grade class, a new teacher/principal came to White Elementary. Her name was Miss Anna Lou Sharp; she would become a legend. Earl told Ted White, his buddy, that they could run her off too. Miss Sharp was a short stoutly built woman who wore nice dresses and always smelled of perfume, but she couldn't be "run off." Her punishment consisted of bending a student over her desk, giving the student 15 licks "dipping at the knees and following through like Babe Ruth hitting a home run." After the 15th lick, she would hug you to her ample chest. Smelling her "honeysuckle" perfume convinced Earl he wanted to be a teacher.

Earl only got two whippings from Miss Sharp who had little trouble establishing and maintaining control. One day Earl heated a metal chair against the pot bellied stove and offered it to Betty White as she and the other students came in out of snow. It got a good laugh as she jumped out of the chair and got Earl's second and last paddling from Miss Sharp.

Miss Sharp was a strict teacher who required her students to read the classics and memorize poems like "The

Raven" by Edgar Allen Poe. Mr. Hoffmeister said he always responded to questions about students being cheated by being in split-level class by recounting how much he learned listening to all the three-grades lessons. He credits Miss Sharp with instilling true values in him and always challenging him to do things he did not believe he could do. He said that he's always regretted not going back to White Elementary to thank her.

One incident concerning Miss Sharp is a good example of how a teacher in those days had to act not to be run off from a school. (Many of us who worked in outlying rural schools had similar experiences.) One day a boy who had dropped out of high school started hanging around the school during lunch time and harassing the students. Miss Sharp told him to leave. He replied very defiantly that he would leave when he got good and ready. Miss Sharp quietly turned and went into the school. She returned with a baseball bat. Earl laughs as he recalls Miss Sharp chasing the boy swinging the baseball bat. He never came back.

EARL HOFFMEISTER KNOX COUNTY SCHOOLS SUPERINTENDENT

Young High School Memories

Coach Cecil Stone. An Inspiration to his Students who gave his life in WW II service.

Young High Basketball Team Captain, Earl Hoffmeister.

Earl Hoffmeister, Football Star. Sports were a passion for Earl.

Elected Mr. Young High School by student body. He was elected football captain of '44 and voted outstanding basketball player of '45.

Chapter 2
Young High School

In the fall of 1941, Mr. Hoffmeister entered Young High School as a Freshman. He recalls his first day as an absolute disaster. "It all started when I got on the bus; I was real bashful with girls, and the loudest, most vivacious girl I had ever seen plopped down by me and started talking non-stop. It was the longest bus ride of my life, and I swore I would not ride that bus again."

The second disaster of the day was the temperature; it was close to 90 degrees by early afternoon and air conditioning had not even been thought of. Mrs. Hoffmeister had dressed him out in new trousers which were 75% wool. Earl pointed out that 75% scratchy wool trousers and 90 degree weather did not go together. He also had on a brand new pair of shoes. The floor had just had a concrete sealer put on them, and his shoes sounded like suction cups every step he took.

Foremost in his mind was how to get through the day and not have to sit by that high spirited girl on the way home. He decided that if he went out for both football and basketball he would never have to sit with that girl again. He could hitchhike home after practice. Earl was confident he could do it as his brother had only weighed 130 pounds and had made it as a guard the previous year.

So that afternoon he reported to Coach Wade Keever who told the new players to run down the field on every play and hit the man catching the ball. Earl went down the field at full speed and tore into his first team star back. Earl was amazed when the coach chewed him out. Earl had tackled him before he got the ball.

John Clabo had transferred from Carter High because Carter High had quit playing basketball during the war. Like Earl, he had wanted to play both sports. John weighed 210 pounds and had been the fastest man on the Carter football team. Coach Keever started him as fullback. Gene Huff was the defense guard and he hollered, "Look boys, fresh meat." Several minutes later when he recovered he had a sheepish grin on his face; Clabo had run over him.

John and Hoffmeister's brother were great friends; they often double dated in a 1931 A Model Ford. John and Earl were captains of the Young High football team. They were together three years in high school and four years in college. John was drafted during his last year of high school and served in the Marines. He boxed most of his career.

John and Earl also coached one year at Inman High School together and that year their team was the district champion. Later John Clabo became football coach at Powell High School before returning to his old school Young High to become football coach there. Hoffmeister still praises John Clabo as one of the best and most dedicated coaches in Knox County.

Hoffmeister also went out for basketball during his freshman year. Coach Stone was his coach who would sit in a chair letting his manager shoot and Hoffmeister having to rebound hour after hour, day after day. Coach Stone went into the U.S. Marines during Hoffmeister's second year. Coach Stone was killed in the Pacific. Hoffmeister tried even harder to be what Coach Stone wanted him to be. Earl credits Coach Stone as being responsible for his being offered eight scholarships in basketball and football from the University of Tennessee, Clemson, Kentucky, Wofford College and two or three other colleges. But Earl's plans for college were interrupted by Uncle Sam.

In July of 1945, when Earl was 18 years old, he was drafted into the Army where he spent 1½ years training mules. Hoffmeister always grins when he reckons this was an excellent background for education. He was sent to Fort Sill, Oklahoma, which was an artillery base where he trained mules to carry artillery in mountainous regions. His outfit was then transferred to the regular Army at Fort Bragg, North Carolina, and he finished his service as Head Mechanic in the Division of Trucks.

Earl in Army uniform.

After his military obligation was fulfilled, he turned his attention to taking advantage of the college scholarships and decided to go to the University of Tennessee. Earl was eager to go to U.T. to play for General Robert Neyland. Coming from a small school of 500 students, U.T. was overwhelming. Most of Earl's teammates from Young High School had been playing on the first team since they were 16; they quickly realized that at U.T., they were going to be blocking dummies for the next three years. Maybe, they would make the first team when they were seniors.

Coach Phil Dickens, a former U.T. great, had been hired at Wofford College, which was one of the top academic schools in the nation requiring four years of Latin or Greek. Fortunately Hoffmeister confesses that Spanish became an alternative before he enrolled. Hoffmeister, John Clabo, Harvey Moyers, Gene Huff, Elrod Cheatham, Bob Pollard, Bob Dunn, Jack Beeler and Charles Webb all transferred to Wofford so they would have a better chance of playing in their first two years. Unfortunately, in the middle of the first year, the conference ruled that they were ineligible to play. Everyone expected them to go back to U.T.

But Coach Dickens pleaded with them to stay and helped them to get jobs after school to pay expenses. He got John Clabo and Earl coaching jobs at Inman, South Carolina. Their team won the district championship that year. Of the 11 students that transferred to Wofford from U.T., 10 graduated. Only one returned to Tennessee, and he had to return home because of family problems.

All played football at Wofford and all graduated. These men were to remain friends for a lifetime; several of them ended up in Knox County Schools. The football team won 26 games before they were defeated in a bowl game 13-17 by Florida State. Hoffmeister had many part-time jobs after school and between ball practices. He taught older people to drive, worked on cars and trucks, worked as a lifeguard. He was even manager of a city park.

Hoffmeister stresses that his mother and dad could have afforded to send him to college, but he was determined to go on scholarships and part-time work, and he succeeded. He graduated in 1951 from Wofford College with a Bachelor of Science Degree in Education. Earl was not only the first in his family to finish high school, he also was the first to graduate from college. His brother finished high school after serving three years in the U.S. Navy.

Earl later gained a Master of Science Degree in Administration and Supervision at U.T. He took an additional 45 hours to certify himself as a principal. He also obtained an Endorsement as a Superintendent.

At Wofford College, Earl set the working patterns for his life; i.e., he always earned extra money by relying on his mechanical skills. During his time at Wofford College, he had a night job at the cotton mill and did mechanical work for different people. When he began his teaching career in Georgia, he continued to do extra jobs and also built himself and JoAnne a home in addition to teaching. When he began teaching in Knox County, he continued to earn extra money by repairing and maintaining typewriters for the system as well as fixing cars and getting into the construction business.

Earl married JoAnne Elledge, August 26, 1950. They met while he was playing football at Wofford; JoAnne had been a cheerleader. Her home was in Spartanburg. JoAnne went to a business college.

Earl was offered a job in Covington, Georgia at the Newton County High School where he also was the coach for girls and boys basketball as well as football. His principal was Homer Sharp who Earl says was one of the most outstanding men he has ever known. Of course, he also taught physical education. In the summer he worked as Assistant Director for the Boy Scouts of America in the Atlanta area. His beginning salary was $2700 a year. He and JoAnne wanted to build a house, but the bank would only loan them enough to build a room and a half. This was the beginning of his construction business. He likes to recall he was able to buy a lot for $500 and build a five room house for $5500.

Principal Homer Sharp.

Earl had been away from his home for almost 10 years when he and JoAnne decided to return to Knox County. Earl applied for a coaching job at Powell High School in 1955. After an initial interview with Mrs. Patterson, he had his first interview with Miss Doyle. Miss Doyle would have known Earl's father from his bus driving days; Hollis had taken

EARL HOFFMEISTER KNOX COUNTY SCHOOLS SUPERINTENDENT

students from Vestal on field trips. After some exchange of pleasantries and getting his teaching job secured, Earl offered to repair and maintain the systems 360 typewriters for $1.00 a piece. That was agreed upon, and the conversation continued for some time. As he was about to leave, Earl asked Miss Doyle if he had worked long enough for her to ask for a raise – 25 cents more on each typewriter. She laughed and agreed and Earl Hoffmeister began his 37 year career in Knox County.

W. W. Morris, Superintendent of Powell High.

Neither would have ever dreamed that this would take him from a physical education and coach to becoming the Superintendent of Knox County Schools.

Earl taught physical education and coached boys basketball for one year at Powell and also football at Powell High School for four. He was twice selected as Coach of the Year – his first year and last year at Powell High. Earl decided to move on to Central High School and teach mechanical and architectural drawing and leave his coaching days behind. One of the reasons for leaving coaching was to free up time so he could spend more time with his family and also be involved more in his construction

Earl McCall, Principal of Powell High.

Dan Boring, Principal of Central High.

business. His partner in the construction business was J.D. Jett, and they built numerous houses in the area including five in the suburb where JoAnne and Earl still live.

JoAnne and Earl have had three children – Dan, David and Debbie. Their lives have not been untouched by tragedy. Their son Dan died in a car accident on his way to classes at Lincoln Memorial University at Harrogate in March of 1975. To compound the tragedy, Earl's father died the same day that Dan was buried.

Dan Hoffmeister.

Shortly after being elected Superintendent, David's young wife Jenny, who was only 20 was found dead in bed at home. Her husband David found her after he returned from a fishing trip. The examining physician told them that the death was caused by a blood clot in the heart.

David and Jenny had been married since 1972, and they were parents of a son, Jason. David was already in construction and land development where he would continue. Earl and JoAnne with support from other family members helped David to care for Jason. Jason is now finishing his Masters Degree in Occupational Therapy. His wife Michelle is completing her B.S. in Nursing.

David and wife Jenny.

Jason, son of David and Jenny, with his bride Michelle.

Deborah and her husband Gerald Johnson and their son Will.

Deborah Anne, Earl and JoAnne's daughter, is married to Gerald Johnson who works at Oak Ridge. Deborah attended Hiawasee College and is employed as a Resource Aide at Adrian Burnette Elementary in Knox County. She and Gerald are the parents of Will Daniel Johnson who is majoring in Latin at the University of Tennessee.

Another important family member is Hoffmeister's only sibling – his older brother H. L. Hoffmeister, Jr., with whom Earl has always been very close. Earl followed H.L. through school until H.L. was drafted into the Navy. They were both outstanding athletes. Earl always tells about H.L. being a first string guard on Young High's football team in spite of only weighing 130 pounds. Earl is also very proud of the work ethic in the Hoffmeister family. After H.L. got out of the Navy, he finished his G.E.D. and went to business college. He worked for Crane Plumbing Company for 47 years until he retired without missing a day. I suspect that Earl's work record would also be exemplary.

Earl and his brother H.L. in his Navy uniform.

Chapter 3
The Election of 1976

As the time drew closer for the election of 1976, there was a general feeling throughout Knox County that it was time for a change. Miss Doyle had been Superintendent of Schools for 30 years since 1946. Stories had circulated since the 1972 election that she would not run again, but was determined to pick her successor. One story was told that she had identified Don Steiner who had served as principal in the Carter Community – Elementary and High School – as her successor. But that story and prediction came to an end when Don Steiner died in 1974.

Miss Doyle had also acted out of character by getting involved in some state and city political contests. In 1974, she had campaigned vigorously in the Republican gubernatorial primary for Dr. Nat Winston who lost to Lamar Alexander. Then to many peoples surprise, she accepted a chairship in the mayoral campaign for the incumbent Kyle Testerman who also lost to Randy Tyree. She also had been involved in the election campaigns of some County Court members as well.

Moreover, in the later summer of 1975, Miss Doyle publicly announced that she planned to retire when her term of office expired. She told one of the local newspapers that she wanted to run for a position on the Knox County Quarterly Court. Her brother, father and grandfather had served in that position.

Based on her announcement to retire, the Knox County Education Association began a campaign to raise money to buy Miss Doyle a Cadillac as a tribute to her contributions. It was believed that Miss Doyle had selected Beecher Clapp to run in the Republican Primary for Superintendent. Certainly Beecher Clapp and other members of the Central Office believed it. Mr. Clapp, who had been in the Knox County Schools as a teacher, principal and supervisor since the 1950's seemed an ideal choice. He was highly qualified having graduated from the Teachers College, Columbia and done his graduate work at U.T. Mr. Clapp was devoted to Knox County Schools and spent almost as much time as Miss Doyle did at that job. But Beecher was not a political animal; he was not a back slapper; he was not "a good old boy." Party leaders could not be persuaded that Mr. Clapp could be elected.

The party leaders put stress on having a strong candidate in the Superintendent race because the Democrats had gained the Mayor's office as well as the Governor's office. No one else that had emerged could win. She had to run and by mid or late November, she had decided to do just that. It had come down to party loyalty; she could not stand the thought of the Democrats getting that office as well.

But there was the complication of that gold Cadillac scheduled to be presented to Miss Doyle on December 1, 1975. The presentation was at Doyle High School named in her honor, and it was celebrated to a standing room only gathering. Colleagues celebrated the Superintendent's successes in office by recalling her numerous accomplishments over the past 30 years, telling stories of numerous encounters with Miss Doyle; there were even some poems recited by people who had written them. At the end of the presentation after the gold Cadillac had been bestowed, Billy K. Nicely, principal of Doyle High School let the cat out of the bag stating that there was no reason Miss Doyle couldn't drive it for the next four years as Superintendent!

To quell the rumors that the Cadillac was a retirement gift – and everyone knew it was – the Chairmen of the Knox County Education Association, Edith McNabb and Jim Bellamy sent a letter to the editor of the *Knoxville News-Sentinel* stating that it was planned all along as a birthday present – and not a retirement gift. But the public wouldn't buy it. A little more than two months later, on February 19, 1976, Miss Doyle announced that she would seek reelection as Knox County School Superintendent. Miss Doyle was quite candid in explaining why she changed her mind. She admitted that she had been told by political leaders and even by the principals in Knox County that Beecher couldn't be elected. "He's just not the kind of folk that can get down on the level of common people." The leaders in the Republican Party insisted that she run again. And so she did.

That announcement was welcomed by some, but not without some qualms. Many people could not believe she could be defeated; many could not even imagine anyone seriously challenging her at the polls. But Miss Doyle was 72, there had been the expectation of her retiring and there were a lot of people who were ready for a change.

But early in 1976, a name began to emerge of someone who was considering running for Superintendent; that name was Earl Hoffmeister, an assistant principal at Central High School. Few people had any idea who he was or why he thought an assistant principal of a city school could be elected Superintendent of Knox County Schools. He had been with the Knox County and Knoxville City Schools having stayed at Central after it was annexed by the city since 1955; but he had no county wide administrative experience. He had never even been a full principal. Mr. Hoffmeister certainly had no name recognition from holding any public office. There was even a question of whether he had or could get a Superintendent's Certificate in time to run before the primaries or even the election itself. And, at first, the rumor mill circulated the story he was going to run against Miss Doyle in the Republican Primary and then the story emerged that no, he was going to run as a Democrat.

EARL HOFFMEISTER KNOX COUNTY SCHOOLS SUPERINTENDENT

One of the early new stories to appear confirming Mr. Hoffmeister's intention to run was in the *Knoxville News Sentinel*, February 2, 1976. He stated that he expected to announce his candidacy around March 1. He was quoted as saying that he was a school man and not a politician, and that he did not expect the campaign to be easy. Mr. Hoffmeister also stated that he had nothing against Miss Doyle, but that he believed the school system needed a change and a younger superintendent.

When questioned about his chances of being elected, he said he was willing to take his chance of getting his ears pinned back. Mr. Hoffmeister also stated that he had been a winner all his life, and that Miss Doyle could be beaten. In the same article, it was reported that Miss Doyle had spoken about her 30 year tenure at the meeting of the Knox County PTA Council. She had also distributed a two-page documented entitled, "A 30-Year Comparative Study" listing the growth and improvements in the school system during her tenure. The article also reported that several people at the meeting said that they had signed the qualifying petition for her during the past week.

In the meanwhile, Mr. Hoffmeister had little success getting the Knox County Election Commission to allow him to run. The qualifying deadline for candidates to run for their party's nomination was March 25. Hoffmeister had filed his petition to run in the Republican Primary only to have it turned down because he did not have a Superintendent's Certificate from the State Board of Education. The deadline for the Democratic Primary also passed with Hoffmeister not being able to get on the ballot, but the Tennessee Election Commission, Shirley Hassler, said it would still be possible for him to run in the August election.

The *Knoxville Journal's* story of May 13, 1976 really summed up the certificate qualifying procedures, and what numerous officials including Warren Webster, Chairman of the Knox County Republicans had to say with its headline, "Hoffmeister's School Race on Confusion." The legislature and Governor Ray Blanton had become involved because of a similar problem in Spenser, Tennessee, according to State Representative Shelby Rhineart of Spenser. He had introduced a bill to clear up a problem there where a Superintendent had been elected without a certificate. This bill intended to set the date for submitting the certificate by September 1, 1976 – the date on which the superintendent would take office moving it from the date set by the Election Commission prior to the primaries. But the bill was withdrawn after it had been defeated by the Legislature.

However, to further complicate the situation, the State Board of Education waived its regulations for a Morgan County candidate for superintendent who "had all but wrapped up his work for the certificate," according to Don England, Director of the State Board of Certification. Obviously, the Board's action in that situation had to apply to Mr. Hoffmeister who also had "all but completed his work" at U.T. for his certificate. And so May saw the end of the certificate controversy. But the deadline for running in the Democratic Primary had also passed, and Mr. Hoffmeister was unable to get on the ballot. He won the Democratic Primary by a write-in vote that also gave him enough votes to qualify.

Early in 1976, Mr. Hoffmeister had decided to run; he had considered it several months before because it was believed that Miss Doyle was going to retire and several people, including Al Bell, Charlie Webb and John Clabo had urged him to run. But most of his fellow teachers were very surprised when he told them his intentions. One of the first people that he spoke to was Jean Payne, a fellow teacher at Central High that Mr. Hoffmeister had admired since 1958 as an outstanding teacher of civics, history and government. Jean was really surprised when he told her of his plans as she had no idea that he had ever thought of running for public office. Earl had never shown much interest in politics or even in professional organization. His job as an educator and building houses as a second vocation certainly had kept him busy.

She was even more surprised when he asked her to be his campaign manager. Jean Payne had as much experience running a political campaign as Earl had in running for political office.

Today, they both describe the whole undertaking as a grass roots campaign. But from an initial start of Jean Payne and a handful of high school students, a winning campaign emerged with all the components in place – committees, platform, brochures, speaking engagements and dedicated volunteers mailing out cards, phone surveys and the like. Little official support from the official Democratic Party showed itself in the early stages, but gradually folks began to believe that Mr. Hoffmeister might actually have a chance.

Help came mostly from individuals – Boyd Cloud was one of the strongest supporters along with others like Paul Monger, Robert Watson, Margaret and Reed Garrison, Nora and Ab de Armond, and Mary Sue Miller. Even the Reverend J. B. Mull and his wife were instrumental in getting four billboards erected. The campaign was kept totally positive at Mr. Hoffmeister's insistence. He was often quoted as saying that you don't attack a lady. The campaign centered around "Time for a Change" and "Now You Have a Choice." By and large, very few of Knox County or Knoxville City educators came out openly for Mr. Hoffmeister. The most notable exceptions were Jean Payne, Al Bell, Nora De Armond from

Cedar Bluff and Tommy Schumpert. Tommy Shumpert said his first ever political action was writing a letter of support for Mr. Hoffmeister.

At the beginning of the campaign – and it was a short campaign – Hoffmeister's main issue was maintenance of school buildings, but it soon became apparent that the hot issue, particularly in West Knox County area was open space. The teachers hated it and the parents hated it. But mainly it was just a prevailing and county-wide feeling of the need for a change. So Hoffmeister's lack of experience and his lack of pretense offset one another. People liked him; they believed he could lead the county schools.

One curious event, I believe, set off some rumors and reinforced the belief that somehow Miss Doyle had no intention of losing control of Knox County Schools. Many people were well aware that she planned to hand pick whoever followed her. On June 2, 1976, Dr. Fred Bedelle, Deputy Superintendent of the Knoxville City Schools, was appointed to Knox County Schools at Miss Doyle's request. Part of his duties would be to replace Charles M. Daugherty who was retiring as of July 1. Miss Doyle stated that his other duties would be outlined later.

Dr. Bedelle's appointment raised a lot of eyebrows and questions. Was he going to be groomed to take over as superintendent in 1980 based on the assumption that Miss Doyle would be elected in August 1976? Was this part of Miss Doyle's plan to continue control of Knox County Schools infinitum? But the most damaging rumor was widely circulated and speculated about – would Miss Doyle somehow hand over the superintendency of Knox County Schools to Dr. Bedelle sometime after she was elected. Miss Doyle actually publically denied that one saying she never failed "to finish any game."

EARL HOFFMEISTER KNOX COUNTY SCHOOLS SUPERINTENDENT

The only really negative tactic to surface in the campaign was a particularly vicious letter attacking Miss Doyle personally. Mr. Hoffmeister firmly and emphatically denied any knowledge of it and roundly criticized anyone involved in the writing of the letter. I personally knew of no one who believed that Mr. Hoffmeister was involved. I never heard one critical comment of Mr. Hoffmeister concerning Miss Doyle before, during or after the election.

During the campaign, Miss Doyle voiced criticism of her opponent related to poor attendance at board meetings, professional meetings and even his voting records which revealed no participation in the primaries or the general elections. But Mr. Hoffmeister said from the beginning that he was a school man and not a politician. He basically criticized open space and general subjects like discipline and drugs in the schools. Mr. Hoffmeister was a hard man to confront; he had a natural manner of defusing situations. In one debate, Miss Doyle asked him if she hadn't seen him at the Lincoln Day Dinner – probably meaning to make a point of him being willing to run on either ticket. But Mr. Hoffmeister killed the opportunity by replying that Abraham Lincoln was one of his favorite presidents.

Only one incident really rankled Mr. Hoffmeister, and he has referred to it numerous times through the years. But each time he recounts it, it is like it happened yesterday and he has never told me about it before. In the summer of 1976, Mr. Hoffmeister was asked to come to a graduate class at U.T. to discuss his candidacy for superintendent. One of the supervisors on leave from the Knox County Central Office was in that class. She evidently was determined to embarrass or humiliate him. I doubt that she achieved her objective; but she insured she would never be part of his administrative staff. To this day, 30 years later, he never fails to mention her sitting in her red cat suit, dangling her shoe on the end of her foot. No doubt she was sure this would please Miss Doyle.

In an interview with Tommy Schumpert in the summer of 2005, Tommy observed that, like his own campaign against Dwight Kessell years later, Mr. Hoffmeister did not so much win the election as Miss Doyle lost it. Tommy has been friends with Mr. Hoffmeister since 1956 when Mr. Hoffmeister and Dan Boring coached the county team in their yearly game with the city. Tommy was on the county team. Tommy would go on to teach business at Central High School until he went into Knox County Schools Central Office to be the Business Manager for Mr. Hoffmeister almost until Mr. Hoffmeister retired. He later would serve as Knox County Trustee and County Executive for two terms.

Tommy stressed that "with Earl what you see is what you get" and Tommy saw that as a major strength and significance with Mr. Hoffmeister gaining acceptance and trust with people before and after the election. Tommy also stressed that Mr. Hoffmeister treated everyone the same from President Ronald Reagan to the lowest paid food service worker in the system.

And lose the election Miss Doyle did: on August 5, 1976. Over 50,000 Knox Countians cast votes in the election for Superintendent of Schools. Mildred was defeated by her opponent Earl Hoffmeister by an 1130 vote margin; he carried 95 of the 96 precincts.

The unthinkable had happened. For 30 years, supporters of Mildred Doyle had gathered in Central Office to listen to the election returns and then celebrate the victory, and so it was on that night of August 5, 1976. I remember listening in shocked disbelief as the tallies began to foretell defeat . . . no miracle happened . . . the tide did not turn. The long tables of party food remained largely untouched . . . some wept . . . friends and colleagues tried to express their regret to the superintendent who never thought a night like that would come. Miss Doyle looked and later said she felt stabbed in the back. Many of us felt like somehow we had failed her and we were going on to an unknown future with an unknown captain.

The following days were very difficult. One of the wits in Central Office referred to it as our time in purgatory. Losing the election was like a death that got us into this period, and we wouldn't know until September 1, whether we were in for "heaven" or "hell." Many feared the latter; and wondered if Mr. Hoffmeister would be the devil himself bent on getting rid of Miss Doyle's staff and changing everything.

The next morning after the election was worse than the night before as reality set in. Miss Doyle stoically entered the building and went about her work knowing that she had three weeks to vacate her office. Everyone sensed she was determined to make her system and her staff as secure and protected as she could. The opening of schools, plans and meetings shifted into gear and the rumor was that Beecher Clapp had tried to persuade Miss Doyle to include Mr. Hoffmeister in those plans and meetings. But Miss Doyle would have none of it. By law, she would be Superintendent of Schools until September 1, 1976, and she had no intention of relinquishing one day or one decision.

Miss Doyle spent a lot of time assuring the staff that everything would be all right because the budget was already set, and Dr. Bedelle as Administration Director would be in charge of that budget. So Miss Doyle carried on as superintendent as though nothing was going to change. She was determined that she would make every recommendation for every vacancy for the coming year.

One example of this that I personally recall centered around the retirement of Mattie Campen at Cedar Bluff, one of the schools that had been one of the showplaces of open spaces. The appointment was to be made at the August meeting of the Knox County Schools. For some reason, my name came up as a possible candidate. At the time I was in my third year as a Title I Consultant and Director of the Knox County Reading Is Fundamental Program.

I did have a Principal's Certificate and had been a principal of two schools in Knox County. Initially I considered the position because I had often said and still do that my years as an elementary principal were the happiest years in my career. But accepting that position under these conditions was an insurmountable problem. I believed that Mr. Hoffmeister should make that appointment. I probably would not have accepted the position for other reasons, namely I loved what I was doing and Cedar Bluff was on the opposite side of Knoxville from where I lived.

But suddenly pressure was put upon me to take that position by Dr. Fred Bedelle. He brought all his persuasive powers to bear on me one afternoon shortly before the board meeting was scheduled. But Dr. Bedelle chose the wrong argument to try to change my mind. He stated that after September 1, I would no longer be working for an individual but for a system. I informed Dr. Bedelle that might be true for him, but it would not be true for me. If I couldn't work for Mr. Hoffmeister just as I had for Miss Doyle, I would resign.

Mr. Hoffmeister had his own personal tragedy. The day after winning the election, Mr. Hoffmeister's daughter-in-law, Jeannie, who was only 20 years old died suddenly. Jeannie was David's wife, the mother of a young child, Jason, who was 14 months old. Her death came as a total shock; there had been no warning of the problem that killed her. So, the Hoffmeisters who should have been celebrating an incredible victory were instead plunged into a time of mourning.

Mr. Hoffmeister had gone into Miss Doyle's office to ask her about coming into the office to meet with her. But Mr. Paul Nicely, head of maintenance, had been in Miss Doyle's office. Mr. Hoffmeister told Miss Doyle the reason he had run was sitting in her office and accused Mr. Nicely of "stealing Knox County blind." Incensed Mr. Nicely denied the accusation and stormed out of the office. That ended any more discussion. Mr. Nicely resigned and Mr. Hoffmeister would later institute a full audit of the maintenance department.

On August 29, Lois Thomas wrote an article accompanied by a photograph showing Miss Doyle with boxes behind her desks filled with memorabilia of 30 years. The article described Miss Doyle's trademark of using green ink for general note taking and rough drafts of her speeches. She used green ink to write everything but her official signature. It was reported that Miss Doyle requested that the clerical staff remove every pen that used green ink from Central Office.

Mr. Hoffmeister was later quoted as saying he could have benefitted greatly could he have consulted her on various school matters. But Miss Doyle never got over her bitterness of losing the election and never made her wealth of knowledge available to him.

Looking back over that election especially, Mr. Hoffmeister wished everyone that had made it happen could be listed and thanked as well as all the details included. But he realized that the biography would be mainly a long list of wonderful folks.

Chapter 4
The Beginning of a New Era

Earl Hoffmeister's memory of his first day as Superintendent of Knox County Schools includes his usual recall of a humorous event instigated by him and at his expense. This involved an unsuspecting secretary at Central Office named Jeanna Findley. Mr. Hoffmeister stopped by her desk after getting off the elevator and asked if she knew if they were hiring anyone that day. She had no idea who he was and was no doubt puzzled by his question and told him that she didn't think so. But she did direct him to Beecher Clapp's office as he requested. She was mortified when he later returned to her desk with Beecher Clapp who introduced her to Mr. Hoffmeister, the new Superintendent. But it set the tone for Mr. Hoffmeister's friendliness and naturalness that would be his trademark. And the story became one of his favorites. Mr. Hoffmeister was then taken around and introduced by Beecher to various members of Central Office.

He let everyone know that he considered the staff the best in the state, and he had no plans to change anything. He made no pretense at knowing the details of being superintendent. As Tommy Schumpert and others pointed out as they came to know him, his strength as a leader was to let the staff do what they did best.

Mr. Hoffmeister made no staff changes. To the amazement of everyone, he asked Faye Cox, who had been Miss Doyle's secretary for years to remain in that position. He told Faye he needed her much more than she needed him. His faith in Faye was well placed and she remained his secretary

EARL HOFFMEISTER KNOX COUNTY SCHOOLS SUPERINTENDENT

until he retired. When more secretarial help was needed, he asked Faye to pick someone for the job. Faye picked Elizabeth Wells known for her friendliness and tact.

Mr. Hoffmeister also told Doris June who had been Mrs. Patterson's secretary as well as Faye that they were to do anything for Miss Doyle and Mrs. Patterson that they needed or asked for. Mr. Hoffmeister was not the least bit bothered by various Central Office staff members who had close ties to Miss Doyle and Mrs. Patterson. Miss Doyle's sister-in-law, Jane Humble Doyle, was the Supervisor of Social Studies. He just seemed to take it for granted that all of them supported Miss Doyle in the election and that was the right thing to do.

Faye Cox - Secretary for Miss Doyle and Mr. Hoffmeister.

There was only one job role that he changed. There had been a woman named Ella Mae Jack who had worked for over 20 years. No one seemed to be sure what she did. But on the first day, Mr. Hoffmeister was in the office, she brought him coffee on a silver tray. He was surprised to say the least, but so was she because Mr. Hoffmeister didn't drink coffee. When Mr. Hoffmeister was unable to find out what she did except make coffee for Miss Doyle and Mrs. Patterson and "tidy up," Mr. Hoffmeister found a new job for her in the media center and she left shortly after.

So until January 1977, Mr. Hoffmeister changed no job role except that one and brought no new persons into the Central Office. But he had approached Dan Boring at Central High School soon after he was elected and asked Dan about talking to Tommy Schumpert about the Business Manager's job at Central Office. Tommy agreed to undertake it at the end of the first term in January. Up until January, Dr. Fred Bedelle had been in that position. Mr. Hoffmeister and Fred had known each other many years. Fred did not have the full trust of Mr. Hoffmeister. There were still rumors that Fred was Miss Doyle's direct source of information and most people had heard that she had planned to maintain some control of Knox County Schools through Dr. Bedelle.

Fred remained part of the inner circle in the office, but it was obvious that Mr. Hoffmeister wanted someone in the Business Office in whom he had complete faith. That person was Tommy Schumpert. Tommy had taught Business classes at Central High School; he and Earl had been friends since 1956 when Earl had coached the county team for the traditional City-County Game. As Mr. Hoffmeister still asserts, that was the smartest move he ever made. Tommy would be Business Manager for Knox County Schools until 1990 – 14 years which Tommy described as the job with the most work and the most satisfaction of any position he ever had. In no time at all, Tommy had gained the confidence and trust of the Central Office Staff. Tommy would go on to serve Knox County as Knox County Trustee from 1990-1994 and Knox County Executive from 1994-2002, both elected offices.

Mr. Hoffmeister always laughs recalling Tommy's first day on the job. Tommy and Lawrence Major unloaded a railroad box car of copy paper – 12 hours of hot, backbreaking work. Tommy commented to Lawrence that he was not sure that he was going to like his Central Office job! Hoffmeister added that no one could have had a finer or more loyal person – and also mentioned how loved and respected he was by the entire staff.

Mr. Hoffmeister made a wise choice in depending on Mr. Clapp in instructional matters as well as in other areas.

EARL HOFFMEISTER KNOX COUNTY SCHOOLS SUPERINTENDENT

Beecher had been in the Central Office since the late 1950's serving as Director of Instruction. When Beecher had joined the Central Office staff at the old Hill Avenue location, there had been less than 15 supervisors; when Mr. Hoffmeister took office there were over 36 and additional resource consultants, psychologists, social workers and many other specialists. Mr. Clapp proved invaluable at helping Mr. Hoffmeister understand how these parts fit together.

Before Mr. Hoffmeister took office in September, Mr. Clapp had requested and received job descriptions from most of the supervisors in the Central Office. The stack of documents still clipped together with a handwritten note to "Mr. H. Here are the job descriptions as requested. BEC". It is doubtful that Mr. Hoffmeister spent much time studying them as he got to know his staff and their job roles chiefly by listening.

By the time Mr. Hoffmeister became Superintendent, the organization and the school curriculum had undergone some rapid and controversial changes. Under the leadership of Mrs. Patterson and Mr. Clapp, Knox County had adopted the middle school concept and had created seven middle schools. So schools were basically organized K-5, 6-8, 9-12, but growth problems in West Knox County were already modifying the K-5 organization.

Another reorganizing effort that had an impact in curriculum as well as the organization of the school year was the Extended School Year (ESY) program that had been instituted at Farragut High School 1974-1975 as an attempt to eliminate wasted time and space by using buildings throughout the year. ESY ended at the end of two years because there were not enough students to make three terms feasible.

Accompanying the ESY plan as an essential part was a long term, large scale curriculum development plan to create a standardized curriculum to be used at all grade levels county-wide focusing on the mastery of basic skills. Over 300 people were involved in organizing the curriculum into 45 day modules to fit the extended school year. It was slated to be completed in 1978-79, so it was still in progress when Mr. Hoffmeister came into office.

Instructional strategies facilitating the controversial open space concept were also still in place, as was individualized instruction and team teaching. But walls began to go back up and the traditional classroom began to emerge. There was a wide array of supplementary programs in the school, and Mr. Hoffmeister wisely stepped aside and let people go on with their jobs.

Beecher Clapp as Director of Instruction had the overall responsibility for planning, developing and evaluation of all system-wide curriculum as well as being involved in overseeing and monitoring all instructional programs and other complementary activities and areas. Mr. Clapp directed, supervised and coordinated instructional staff and services. There were separate supervisors for elementary, middle and secondary instruction. When Mr. Hoffmeister became superintendent, the city and county shared Mrs. Ruth Sams as Kindergarten Supervisor. By the time Mrs. Sams returned to the City School System in 1978, Kindergarten in Knox County became the responsibility of the Elementary Supervisors and Mrs. Sams had married Beecher Clapp.

Beecher Clapp.

EARL HOFFMEISTER KNOX COUNTY SCHOOLS SUPERINTENDENT

Earl and his Kitchen Cabinet: Dr. Fred Bedelle, Tommy Schumpert, Earl, Dr. Richard Yoakley, Jim Robinson and Beecher Clapp.

Ruth Clapp, Kindergarten Supervisor for both Knox County and Knoxville City.

The elementary supervisors were Willa Silvey, Mary Jo Husk and LaNoka Rhodes; Willa and Mary Jo had been in the Central Office a long time; Lanoka was a relative new comer. During Mr. Hoffmeister's tenure, Lanoka would advance to Elementary Coordinator and Willa and Mary Jo would retire and be replaced by Dr. Anne Meek and Sue Boyer.

Dr. Anne Meek.

BENNA F. J. VAN VUUREN

Lanoka Rhodes.

Mary Jo Husk.

Sue Boyer.

Willa Silvey.

Elizabeth Wells,
Earl's secretary.

EARL HOFFMEISTER KNOX COUNTY SCHOOLS SUPERINTENDENT

Bob Goff, Supervisor of Middle School Education.

Dr. William Phifer, Supervisor of Secondary Education.

The middle school supervisor was Bob Goff who had followed Martha Jean Bratton in 1975 when she took maternity leave and went on to complete her doctorate. Mr. Goff had served as principal of Doyle Middle prior to his coming to the Central Office. Mr. Goff would remain in that position throughout Mr. Hoffmeister's 16 year tenure.

The Supervisor of Secondary Education throughout Mr. Hoffmeister's four terms was Dr. J. W. Phifer. Dr. Phifer pointed out in his job description that although he worked with all principals related to curriculum, he mainly worked with the principals who were designated the "Curriculum Principal." It should be pointed out that all principals were directly responsible to the superintendent.

Mr. Hoffmeister certainly came into a complex organization from a background of being an assistant principal of another school system; it was an amazing phenomena to begin with and even the skeptics had to admit he was successful. Just

Virginia Underwood, Reading.

Charlene De Ridder, Mathematics.

gaining an understanding of the numerous supervisors and the how and why of their jobs was a challenge.

The subject area supervisors were a good example of the complexity of how schools were operated. When Hoffmeister became superintendent in 1976, there were eight subject area supervisors. Except for Virginia Underwood, all were responsible for their specific subject K-12. Virginia Underwood as Reading Supervisor was responsible for the Developmental Learning Program K-8 initially funded for Title I Schools. This included managing a reading center and supervising several traveling reading teachers.

Charlene De Ridder was the Knox County Mathematics Supervisor who was responsible for the K-8 math continuum as well as the high school mathematics program. This was divided into General Mathematics, Applied Mathematics, Algebra I, Geometry, Algebra II and Advanced Mathematics.

Sarah Simpson, who would become Director of Instruction and later Assistant Superintendent, was the Language Arts Supervisor when

Sarah Simpson, Language Arts.

EARL HOFFMEISTER KNOX COUNTY SCHOOLS SUPERINTENDENT

Mr. Hoffmeister became superintendent. Sarah was one of the two people that Mr. Hoffmeister had met previously; her husband Doc Simpson, had been a coach in the Knox County schools. After Doc's early death due to Lou Gehrig's disease, she devoted her time and energy to Knox County Schools - becoming an icon. But in 1976, in addition to the Language Arts Curriculum, Sarah was also responsible for Foreign Language.

The Social Studies Supervisor in 1976 was Jane Humble Doyle who had been the widow of a minister until she had married Miss Doyle's brother a few years previously. Jane would take early retirement in 1978 intending to attend seminary only to develop and die from brain cancer. She would be replaced by Al Bell, a teacher from Powell High School, who had served as a County Commissioner and had been very instrumental in persuading Mr. Hoffmeister to run for superintendent. Al would continue as Social Studies Supervisor throughout Mr. Hoffmeister's tenure.

Jane Humble Doyle, Social Studies.

Bob Chambers was the Science Supervisor for K-12 in Knox County Schools. He also was responsible for Environmental Programs which was a big thing in the 1960's and 1970's. Fifth grade students were encouraged to spend

Bob Chambers, Science.

a week at an environmental camp; one was located at Townsend and another one near Middlesboro.

VaLera Lewis was the Art Supervisor at the time Mr. Hoffmeister became Superintendent. She had been in the Central Office since the 1950's. One great memory I have of her was when she persuaded Miss Doyle to hire an outside contractor to paint Asbury School in 1962 when I became principal. Val convinced him with my help to paint the classrooms egg-shell blue, pink, lime green – everything but "Knox County Green." She and I then talked him out of all of his left over cans of enamel paint. She and I and teachers and students painted the hook racks in the hall, cabinets, etc. a rainbow of psychedelic colors! Mr. Nicely, Maintenance Supervisor, almost had a stroke when he came out. But lots of people came to see what bright colors could do to an old school. Fred Patterson became Art Supervisor later during Hoffmeister's term.

In Memoriam: VaLera Muse Lewis
1916 - 1996

The name she inherited from her parents forecast her vocation. A Muse, in greek mythology, was a guiding spirit for the arts. For Miss VaLera Muse, it was visual art that captivated her and ordained her to share her fascination with students.

Val's formal preparation for teaching began in 1933 in her home state at the University of Oklahoma, continued with the BA Degree in 1941 at Oklahoma East Central College, and culminated in her adopted state with the Master's Degree in Art at the University of Tennessee in 1971.

During that span of years, she also married Doyle Dick Lewis, taught art education in Oak Ridge from 1944 until taking leave to care for son Ricky in 1949, and returned to teaching at Knoxville Central High School in 1955. She became Knox County's first traveling art teacher in 1955 and was elevated to the position of Art Supervisor in 1964. In that position, Val saw the art program grow to twenty-seven art specialists in eleven elementary schools, nine middle schools and seven high schools before her retirement in 1983. To provide guidance for the increasing number of teachers, Val developed Knox County's first written art curriculum. Her many contributions to the lives of hundreds of students and teachers through art bear tribute to the fact that VaLera Muse Lewis lived out the calling of her name.

VaLera Lewis, Art.

EARL HOFFMEISTER KNOX COUNTY SCHOOLS SUPERINTENDENT

J. B. Lyle, Music.

J. B. Lyle was the Supervisor of Choral and Instrumental music during the time Mr. Hoffmeister was superintendent. At the time Mr. Hoffmeister was elected there were 50 music teachers; some of them traveled between schools.

Carolyn Sullivan, who had been in Central Office several years, described herself as wearing a "three sided" hat. She was Supervisor of Physical Education, Driver Education and Health. She also moved 10 bicycles from school to school for a Bicycle Safety Program and was responsible for securing 90+ cars and insurance for the Driver Education Program. Add field days, school preparedness plans and working with the Red Cross and it could be appreciated that the hardest part was for her to decide which hat to wear and when.

There were several other supervisors that Mr. Hoffmeister had to get acquainted with and their areas of responsibility: Herbert Clement, Vocational Education; Ray Jones also in Vocational Education; Lawrence Majors, Supervisor of Adult Vocational Education; Bruce M. Hinton, Director of Vocational, Adult and Community Education. The list and the job descriptions must have seemed endless.

Carolyn Sullivan, Physical Education, Driver Ed, and Health.

Another key area that had an impact on instruction in Knox County was the Director and Coordinator of Federal Projects – Jim Robinson who was the first African American supervisor in Knox County. Jim served in that role from 1965 all through Mr. Hoffmeister's tenure. Mr. Robinson, like others in his role had a constant battle to ensure that Title I funds were used only for approved Title I projects. Mr. Robinson had a Title I Consultant whose job role was to ensure parent involvement in the planning, development, implementation and evaluation of the Title I Projects. I served in the role of Supervisor of Parent Involvement for the school year 1974-1975 to the end of the 1979-1980 school year. I also was the Knox County Reading Is Fundamental Coordinator.

Benna van Vuuren, Title I and RIF.

There were also support services with their supervisors, including Dr. Richard Yoakley who was Director of Guidance and Psychological Services; William Neal, Supervisor of Special Education; Dr. Sam Bratton, Research and Evaluation; John Hays, Transportation; Lib Hotchkiss, Materials and Library

Dr. Sam Bratton.

Dr. J. B. Bolin, Adult Education.

Bill Orr, Transportation.

Dr. Joseph Chandler.

Services; Dr. J. B. Bolin, Adult Education; Bill Orr, Transportation; Helen Reagan, Food Services; L. E. Turner, Maintenance, Dr. Joseph Chandler, Personnel.

Add 48 members of the Central Office Clerical Personnel, 19 school Psychologists, 11 Social Service workers, 7 in the Vision Program, 5 Home and Hospital Teachers, 16 Speech and Hearing Teachers, 6 Title I Language Development Teachers, a Talents Unlimited Resource teacher and a Safety Officer and you can well understand the number of people coming and going out of the Central Office.

Mr. Hoffmeister has said that his job of repairing the typewriters in the Knox County Schools at least got him into the high schools and many of the elementary schools. Of course, Mr. Hoffmeister had been a Knox County teacher for his first few years until the city had annexed Central High along with a large number of other schools. There had already been an attempt to clarify lines of authority by developing job descriptions and the drawing up of an organizational chart. More work was done on both of these efforts and by 1979, there was a personnel manual and an organization chart.

There were certainly some power struggles before the final ink dried, but basically Beecher Clapp (Director of Instruction), Dr. Fred Bedelle (Administrative Assistant), Dr. Richard Yoakley (Director of Guidance and Psychological Services) and Jim Robinson (Director of Federal Projects) reported directly to Mr. Hoffmeister with perhaps the rest of Central Office divided up among them.

There were also four Head Start Programs with an Administrative Director Jane Madden and seven staff members. The Head Start Center was located at the former Asbury Building. These four Head Start Programs were located at Asbury, Brickey, Dante and Fairview.

Theoretically all the principals were directly responsible to the Superintendent. There were nine high schools in 1976: Byington, Solway, Carter, Doyle, Farragut, Gibbs, Halls, Karns Knox-Union Vocational and Powell. There were seven middle schools: Carter, Cedar Bluff, Doyle, Farragut, Halls, Karns and Powell. And there were 32 elementary schools: Adrian Burnett, Ball Camp, Blue Grass, Bonny Kate, Brickey, Carter, Cedar Bluff Intermediate, Cedar Bluff Primary, Corryton, Fairview, Farragut Primary, Farragut Intermediate, Gap Creek, Gibbs, Green Hill, Halls, Hardin Valley, Heiskell, High Bluff, John Sevier, Karns, Mascot, Mount Olive, New Hopewell, Powell, Ramsey, Ritta, Riverdale, Skaggston, Sunnyview, Vestal and White.

Several of the elementary schools were in dire condition and would close during Mr. Hoffmeister's first term. These would include John Sevier, Mascot and Skaggston which would be incorporated into East Knox, Heiskell, Green Hill and Hardin Valley would go to Fairview or Copper Hill. White and High Bluff would also close shortly afterward.

In an interview with Lois Thomas of the *Knoxville News-Sentinel* shortly before she left office, Miss Doyle had predicted that the new superintendent would face more problems with school personnel, parents, the Board and County Commission than she did. She predicted the Board would become more active, more forceful with Hoffmeister than with her because the Board had relied on her experience. Miss Doyle reminded Miss Thomas and her readers that all the superintendent does is make recommendations – it is the Board that makes decisions.

Mr. Hoffmeister's first experience with the County School Board had been August 18, 1976 – midway between his being elected Superintendent in August and taking office September 1. Miss Doyle stated that she had not conferred with Mr. Hoffmeister on her recommendations because "he is not Superintendent of schools."

Miss Doyle had recommended the Board grant tenure to Dr. Bedelle as Administrative Assistant which would have given him the right to hold that office after Mr. Hoffmeister took over in September. Dr. Bedelle rejoined the county system after an absence of 13 years. Tenure is seldom granted in less than two years. Miss Doyle stressed Dr. Bedelle's knowledge of county court on budget matters and school financing.

Mr. Hoffmeister objected because he was not consulted although the Administrative Assistant "is supposed to be my right arm." He stressed that he knew and liked Fred and that he might even have recommended him, adding "I can't say if

I would or I wouldn't," but he should have been consulted. In a mailogram Mr. Hoffmeister requested that Dr Bedelle not be given tenure or Wayne Smith to be appointed as principal of Cedar Bluff. Mr. Hoffmeister offered no objection to the appointment of Bill Orr, Supervisor of Transportation, Dr. J. B. Bolin as Supervisor of Adult Education or of Lib Hotchkiss, Supervisor of Materials and Library Services.

All the appointments were approved, but Dr. Bedelle was not given tenure. Miss Doyle stated that she was trying to leave the system in good shape and added, "I do not believe that the boys and girls of the system should bear the brunt of promises that were made in the election. . ." Mr. Hoffmeister did respond to that remark, "I came through the campaign without a single promise to any teacher."

In a later interview with Lois Thomas, she defended her actions to have Dr. Bedelle tenured as not enabling her to maintain control over the system. Instead, she insisted it was because the system needed someone who knew what was going on and that Dr. Bedelle was that person. Dr. Bedelle would remain in that position or with that title for the next eight years until he resigned in 1984 and returned to the city, but his duties would continue to be altered, and he was not the Superintendent's "right arm." The first major change would take place in January 1977, with Tommy Schumpert taking over as Business Manager and being Assistant Superintendent August 5, 1981.

Mr. Hoffmeister's first priority after taking office was to straighten out once and for all the Maintenance Department. He insists to this day that had been what motivated him to run for Superintendent in the first place. Mr. Hoffmeister quickly became confident that the rest of Knox County School System would proceed without much of his attention because he believed that the people in supervision knew their jobs and would continue as they had before.

But the Maintenance Department was a "horse of a different color." There were a number of practices he intended to stop immediately, and he intended to have a complete investigation and a detailed audit undertaken. Mr. Hoffmeister had been in construction himself for many years; his brother had worked in a company that was linked to construction; he had a wide circle of friends in Knox County, and he, himself, had experienced the maintenance problem that had not been responded to when he was part of Knox County. So he had heard plenty from all of those sources.

He had made no secret of his intentions and had talked to the Knox County Law Director and to the *Knoxville News-Sentinel* before he made his request for authorization by the School Board. In fact, the story made headlines on the front page of the *Knoxville News-Sentinel* October 5, 1976. The Board reluctantly agreed to the investigation and audit at their October meeting. Board member A. L. Lotts and Paul Hodges were appointed to work with the Superintendent.

Paul Nicely had been the Supervisor of Maintenance for well over 20 years. One newspaper had referred to him as "a long time controversial figure." He was a leading and very active member of the Democratic Party; it was said that Mr. Nicely could "deliver a lot of votes." Many people wondered if that was not why Miss Doyle kept him in his position in the Maintenance Department – maybe she believed she needed those votes to remain Superintendent. It was also rumored that the people in the department were instructed to vote early so that Mr. Nicely could pretty well know that they had voted as instructed.

Principals often grumbled to one another about their inability to get needed maintenance and repair. When the complaints were made to Miss Doyle, they were told that the maintenance budget was not their concern, and Mr. Nicely operated by that budget. Mr. Nicely had already signed another year long contract before Mr. Hoffmeister had taken office. Miss Doyle had stressed even after she was defeated that Dr. Bedelle would be in charge of the budget. Mr. Nicely probably assumed that things would go on as usual.

But with Mr. Hoffmeister there was no stonewalling and changes began immediately. By January, Dr. Bedelle was no longer the Business Manager of Knox County Schools; Tommy Schumpert had replaced him, and the FBI had become involved in the investigation. Paul Nicely was gone from the Maintenance Department and L. E. Turner had been named Supervisor with Lawrence Majors as his assistant. Mr. Turner had been second in command to Mr. Nicely for a number of years, but Mr. Hoffmeister viewed him as an honest and competent man.

By the end of Mr. Hoffmeister's first year, there was a marked improvement in maintenance, and a surplus in the budget. With the staff employed it was not possible to spend what had been appropriated – further proof that something was not right. Maintenance needs had also been assessed and put in priority order, and building programs were underway.

In the meanwhile, the initial investigation had turned up some misuse of federal funds. Mr. Hoffmeister discussed some of the issues with Robert Marshall, Chief of the Knoxville Police and a personal friend. Mr. Marshall helped Earl get the FBI involved with the investigation. Two FBI agents who lived in Knoxville were assigned to work with Mr. Hoffmeister, the two School Board members and other staff members.

Earl even talked his brother into going over invoices looking for discrepancies because of his familiarity with prices for maintenance materials, and he found plenty. Members of the Maintenance Department themselves cooperated once they realized that they would not be held responsible for anything that was uncovered unless they had profited personally. According to Mr. Hoffmeister, witnesses were found that were willing to testify that Knox County trucks and personnel were places they should not have been. For example, Knox County trucks were seen delivering USDA foods twice a week to a private restaurant and even delivered coal to individuals.

A long list of misuse of Knox County trucks and personnel was reported by reliable witnesses concerning the building and equipping of a motel owned by Paul Nicely in Gatlinburg. Trucks were seen unloading materials which included everything from lumber to expensive plumbing supplies and paint and floor covering. Suspicious invoices like the one detailing plumbing supplies such as faucets costing $100 which could not have been used in schools were found, but the many expensive faucets could not be located in any Knox County school.

Knox County personnel who stayed at the Dogwood Motel commented on the cabinets being exactly like the ones found in Knox County schools. A very respected carpenter was willing to testify that not only were he and his crew ordered to build them with Knox County materials, they were also sent to Gatlinburg to install them in bathrooms and kitchens in the motel units. Mr. Hoffmeister said that he believed that the entire motel was built and paid for with Knox County funds.

There were numerous incidents reported of Knox County trucks and personnel being involved in remodeling activities. The activities included painting and similar services as well as repair. A former principal reported he had witnessed a Knox County truck and several workers being used to build a fence on a farm in the Gibbs community.

But it was the area of trying to reconcile invoices and work orders that the greatest discrepancies showed up. The number of invoices from McCalla Wholesale was unbelievable as were the prices Knox County paid on the items. A good example of this was an invoice for numerous flush valves charged at $35 a piece when other companies were selling them at $15. Not only were the prices exorbitant, but the amount of items ordered in one year defied belief. For example, over 300 ladders were purchased in one year and only one could be found at a school. Several sewer machines had been purchased at $300 - $600 a piece and could not be found; a large number of sump pumps were likewise invoiced and were no where to be found. These inflated invoices convinced the FBI that McCalla Wholesale purportedly owned by Paul Nicely and another person was just a front to defraud Knox County.

One of the most astounding instances that was documented occurred when a bulldozer complete with a tractor and trailer to transport it was purchased at a very good saving to Knox County from a salvage sale from the State in Nashville. The whole rig disappeared the same day it arrived in Knox County. It was never reported stolen or accounted for in any way. Mr. Hoffmeister firmly believes that almost 25 years later, he accidentally came across the bulldozer rusting in a field. Mr. Hoffmeister was looking for some land to buy when he spotted it – really much too late to raise questions.

Work orders in the Maintenance Department revealed numerous discrepancies concerning work that was recorded as completed, but physical evidence provided otherwise. School after school was reported as having been painted several times. The FBI lab using a spectagraph could quickly reveal how many coats had been put on a building. For example, according to work orders, Heiskell Elementary had been painted seven times, but the test showed only one coat of paint. Re-roofing schools followed the same pattern; investigators would investigate a roof and only find some tar spread around. Yet, according to work orders, the entire roof had been done. When some of the roofers were questioned, they reported that they were told to take a five gallon can of tar and smear it around in the worse places and so the disclosures went.

Finally the FBI actually presented the evidence to a Grand Jury in a neighboring county successfully and the case was ready to go to court, when one of the FBI agents came to Mr. Hoffmeister's office carrying a box containing all the evidence that had been gathered.

He told Mr. Hoffmeister all he could do was apologize; and the other agent had been taken off the case and recalled to Washington. The FBI would no longer be involved. The agent told Mr. Hoffmeister that in his 20 years in the FBI that this case had been his second most prosecutional case. One of the most incriminating facts uncovered was the U. S. mail had been used in the billing and collecting of fraudulent invoicing. He also stated that he believed that Knox County had lost over $10,000,000. So Mr. Hoffmeister was left with a box - three feet wide, feet wide and a foot deep filled with evidence he could use without the help of the FBI because of local officials who were then in power. He could only reconcile himself with the thought that he could insure a better maintenance program from that day forward. The worst thing for Mr. Hoffmeister to accept was how desperately Knox County Schools needed the maintenance that could have been provided if the department had used the money provided as it was intended.

When Mr. Hoffmeister became Superintendent, some of the schools were in shocking disrepair; some of them were not safe for students to attend. I remember most of the ceiling in one classroom fell in a school one day while I was in the building. Mr. Hoffmeister will always remember the sad state of flat tops; some had grass growing up through the floor when the foundation had shifted; many had cracks, and others leaked. Mr. Hoffmeister recalled the day a storm came through Halls and destroyed a flat top occupied by a teacher and children. Mr. Hoffmeister praised the teacher, the youngest daughter of Earl Woods, who had the foresight to get out of the flat top after one wall had been blown out. She had them crouch next to the foundation with books shielding their heads. Not a wall was left standing, but the teacher and students escaped without serious injury. Mr. Hoffmeister vividly recalls racing to the school and picking up a little girl with her face dirty and tear stained and trying to assure her everything was all right.

Thirty years later it still rankles Mr. Hoffmeister that investigation ended like it did.

One fact that Mr. Hoffmeister was adamant in including was that the FBI stated there was no evidence of Miss Doyle being involved or profiting in any way.

In addition to the Central Office staff and the school staffs, there were at least three other groups to learn the members, procedures and responsibilities — the Knox County School Board with its 9 members, Quarterly Court with its 19 members, and the Tennessee Department of Education with numerous members.

The School Board was known as Miss Doyle's Board and Mr. Hoffmeister found it difficult to deal with it at first. He was well aware that Miss Doyle had encouraged the Board to control the Knox County Schools and be the decision makers. In one of her last interviews she predicted the Board would be more active and stressed that it was Dr. Bedelle who was knowledgeable with the budget and the school system. But Mr.

EARL HOFFMEISTER KNOX COUNTY SCHOOLS SUPERINTENDENT

Hoffmeister intended to be the Superintendent of Knox County Schools and understood politics far more than others believed and he admitted. After being rebuffed by the Board, he made a phone call or two and at the next Board meeting there was standing room only. Mr. Hoffmeister felt that action altered the Board's attitude toward him.

Chapter 5
Politician and Manager

From the beginning of the first campaign, Earl Hoffmeister denied that he was a politician – insisting that he was a school man. If politician meant being part of a political organization or taking part in political campaigns, that was certainly true and Mr. Hoffmeister made no pretense of it. Nor did he allow Miss Doyle to make an issue of it. It's very hard to make an issue of something unless the other candidate denies it or defends his position. And Mr. Hoffmeister did neither.

One of the best examples of this has already been mentioned, but bears being retold. Mr. Hoffmeister was trying to run in the Republican Primary. He attended the Lincoln Day Dinner, but he was unable to run in the Republican Primary and ended up as a write-in candidate in the Democratic Primary – to the consternation of all "real politicians."

Intentional or not, this reinforced Mr. Hoffmeister's image as a "non-politician" and was a smart move even if it was not a planned one. In one debate, Miss Doyle intended to make an issue of him being neither Republican or Democratic by asking him if she hadn't seen him at the Lincoln Day Dinner. Mr. Hoffmeister replied,"Oh, yes ma'am you did. I've always thought that Mr. Lincoln was one of the best presidents we ever had." This not only completely defused that issue, but drew an appreciative chuckle from the audience.

Not a politician? Looking back at that campaign and others, you could draw a different conclusion. There was no one that could have debated Miss Doyle on the Knox County Schools; it would have been comparable to challenging Noah on flood control or ark building and Mr. Hoffmeister never tried. He simply stuck to a low key campaign that never attacked Miss Doyle, except to emphasize it was time for a change and to the voters that now they had a choice. He presented that choice just as he was – a school man, a coach, a scout leader, a family man, but a man who had succeeded in everything he had ever done.

Mr. Hoffmeister was probably not elected on stands he took on issues. Mainly he stuck to what many would have described as so general that they really were non-issues: discipline, better maintenance, new buildings, eliminating drugs in the school. The one hot area that he addressed was the open space concept that was extremely controversial in the schools in West Knox County. Again, there was no in depth analysis, no studies cited. In fact, Mr. Hoffmeister kept his comments so general that after he won the election, he had enough leeway to take a broader view of the open space concept and not to immediately take drastic action. He stated to the newspapers the day after the election that there would be some structured classes next year, but he doesn't plan to do away with the open space concept totally. He said the matter would be carefully studied. The fact was that there were no funds to immediately put up walls and/or modify buildings.

One example of Mr. Hoffmeister's management style was the way he handled and appointed staff to a position. There was a vacancy for a supervisor due to retirement, and the rumor spread that Hoffmeister would appoint the wife of one of his coach friends whose friendship went back to college days. But Mr. Hoffmeister with the recommendation of staff members had decided upon the person he thought was most qualified. Before there was any notification of Hoffmeister's recommendation, the person who had been recommended demanded an interview with Mr Hoffmeister and told him emphatically why he should have that position instead of Mr. Hoffmeister's friend's wife. When he had finished, Mr. Hoffmeister told him the recommendation had already been made. Mr. Hoffmeister did make the comment in telling the incident that if the recommendation had not been made, he might have looked for the second most qualified.

All of Mr. Hoffmeister's personnel appointments did not go smoothly. The first one that backfired occurred in August 1977 less than a year after Mr. Hoffmeister had been in office. Lee Vittatoe, who had been principal of Mascot School for seven years was transferred to Carter Middle School as a teacher. The reasons given were that he did not have a Master's Degree and had no plans for getting one nor did he have a Principal's Certificate nor did he have any plans for getting one.

With the open backing of Miss Doyle, Mr. Vittatoe was represented by Bryan McCarty, the staff attorney for the Tennessee Education Association. Mr. McCarty charged that the Superintendent and the School Board were violating the Private Tenure Act because there was no hearing before the transfer. Mr. Vittatoe was reinstated to an administrative status and regained his $2500 supplement. But he was sent to Carter High School as an assistant intern and given until December 1980 to complete his Master's Degree and his Principal's Certificate.

The August 1977 Board meeting was the only Board meeting that I know that Miss Doyle ever attended after her defeat, and from my point of view I felt she gloated over the outcome. After the meeting, she stopped some members of the staff. I was one of them and I could not believe that she was there to support Mr. Vittatoe. When she stopped me she stated that I must be glad this new guy could not walk over people. I took a deep breath and told her I was not glad – that I had spent the time and money to complete my Master's and get my Principal's Certificate and Lee had not and she knew it. Then she retorted that at least I had sense enough to appreciate the actions of T.E.A. and I told her I was resigning that day. Mrs. Patterson who was with Miss Doyle tried to cool both of us down without much success. Many members of Central Office also resigned that day. My reasons were that I would not accept that T.E.A. should support something or someone that did not meet certification requirements.

Again, Mr. Hoffmeister up until this time in his life had never sought any political power. He was not active in professional organizations and therefore could not cite that he had held any office to which he had been elected. What should have been another issue was not because Mr. Hoffmeister said that he had always had to work additional jobs to support his family – and it's impossible to fault a man for that, particularly a teacher.

Audiences, where there were a few or many, responded to Mr. Hoffmeister's naturalness, his folksiness, and his humor – almost always at his own expense. He wasn't an orator or an entertainer – he was just Earl Hoffmeister. He did not use sarcasm or anything else to belittle others and he gave himself room to maneuver. A good example of this was that he always spoke respectfully of Miss Doyle; even after the election he stressed how much he would value her advice and help.

Another example was at an interview concerning the August 1976 School Board meeting in which Miss Doyle tried to obtain tenure for Dr. Bedelle. In the interview Mr. Hoffmeister stressed that he liked Dr. Bedelle, and that Fred was a good man. Hoffmeister went as far as to say that he might even have recommended him . . . but that he should have been involved. When questioned by the reporter about whether he would have indeed recommend him, Hoffmeister replied that he wouldn't say he would have or he wouldn't say he wouldn't have.

Not a politician? He still talks to everyone he encounters including them as part of whatever is happening. A good example of this was his accompanying the author and Sue Boyer to three locations searching for artifacts for the Museum of Knox County Education. At every place he connected with everyone just as he did when he was superintendent – informally, folksy and humorously, asking each time not to be judged by the company he was with. Later, when he took us for lunch, it was the same. I would guarantee that if he had been running for an office, he would have collected a majority of votes among those folks. He later discovered he had failed to leave a tip for the waitress and drove from Powell to almost Seymour to take the waitress a tip.

This was Mr. Hoffmeister's way of politicking. He recounts how hard it was at the beginning of the first campaign to even hand someone a card and ask them to vote for him. But he was elected and served four terms; and he was a smart enough politician to know when to quit.

In the election of 1980, it was a very different campaign from the campaign of 1976. This time it was Mr. Hoffmeister who was the incumbent. In the Spring primaries two Knox County school people emerged to oppose him — both of them vying to be the nominee on the Republican ballot. One of them was James Monroe, principal of Karns Middle School; the other one was Bill Clabo, football coach at Farragut High. Clabo defeated Mr. Monroe by 3,278 votes.

Bill Clabo and Mr. Hoffmeister ran very positive campaigns. In fact, the newspaper commented on the fact of it being run so politely. Critics raised a question of whether the two men had made some kind of a deal. Clabo flatly denied that saying that nobody would spend the time and money unless he was serious about the job. Clabo said probably that the reports that he and Hoffmeister were in cahoots was the fact that Hoffmeister and his older brother, John, had been friends for years and that they all attended Wofford Collge in South Carolina. In fact, John had just been appointed Head Football Coach at Doyle High School just before the primaries. Hoffmeister denied that the appointment had anything to do with the election. And Clabo received 23,283 votes against Hoffmeister's 31,200 votes which was much higher than Wanda Moody would receive in 1988.

Hoffmeister ran as he had before stating that he was a school man and not a politician. Clabo as the challenger cited general issues such as improvements in reading, organization, and security that could be improved. But there was really no one issue to focus on; Mr. Hoffmeister cited steady improvement in basic skills, maintenance and school construction.

Bill Clabo and Earl Hoffmeister.

Mr. Hoffmeister could also point out that there had been few changes in Central Office Staff since he took office in 1980. After he won the election he stated he had no plans to make any major changes. He stressed the need for work in reading and math skills and taking a firm stand against drug abuse. Asbestos removal also was one of his concerns.

There had also been a rumor that Bill Clabo would be appointed an administrative assistant at Central Office by running against Mr. Monroe. Both men denied that anything like that had even been discussed in any shape, form or fashion. And Mr. Clabo continued working at Farragut and supported Mr. Hoffmeister for the rest of Mr. Hoffmeister's time in office.

But the political climate quickly changed after a referendum to take the city out of the school business after 116 years had passed in 1986. Mayor Kyle Testerman had spearheaded that referendum as a way to release the city and its shrinking tax base from the burden of education. State law required the county to provide educational services to the city pupils. On July 1, 1987, the Knoxville City School System was abolished and the Knox County School System doubled overnight to include a total of 50,000 students, 3,000 teachers and more than 90 schools.

Everyone from the principal of Bearden High School, Edwin Hedgepeth to Carolyn South, President of the Knox County Association agreed that the merger was going well after the 10 month marriage, quoted in a front page article in the West Side Story/Volunteer May 25, 1988. But not everyone was in agreement with that evaluation. By March 14, 1988, Wanda Moody, a member of the Knox County Commission, announced she would run as a Republican for Knox County Superintendent.

EARL HOFFMEISTER KNOX COUNTY SCHOOLS SUPERINTENDENT

Miss Moody made her announcement at the home of her professional roots, Brownlow School, stating that she was ready to help Knox County Schools charge forward into the next generation. Miss Moody had long been involved in education, both at the local and state level. She had served as a teacher, supervisor and member of the superintendent's staff in the Knoxville City Schools. At the state level she had served as Assistant Commissioner of the State Department of Education with Governor Lamar Alexander. At the time she challenged Earl Hoffmeister, she had already served two years as a member of Knox County Commission. Wanda Moody was a formidable challenger; she had an excellent background that certainly qualified her to be superintendent.

Moody's platform centered on improving communication among school personnel, parents, business leaders and the county commission, responsible leadership/management and forward thinking, classroom climate and learning, academics and special emphasis programs, attracting new teachers and streamlining the system to make it truly unified were also included. There was also mention of improved student attendance, a fairer discipline program and reducing the number of Central Office personnel. But the real implication was that Mr. Hoffmeister wasn't capable of being superintendent of a school system that size.

Mr. Hoffmeister had announced his candidacy for the Superintendent of Knox County School as of March 14, 1988 at Powell High School, and this time Mr. Hoffmeister had a vastly different platform and track record to offer from his initial platform of 1976. He chose a campaign slogan: "Communication, Continuity and Commitment" placed as an arrow pointing upward. And he had an impressive track record to present. During his first three terms, he had built, renovated and expanded 17 schools and there were current renovation and building plans in the works. His brochures focused on Educational Features of the Knox County Schools highlighting the demographics of the system . . . serving more than 50,000 students in 90 schools (55 elementary schools, 17 middle schools, 15 high schools, 3 vocational schools and 2 special education centers); supporting 5,157 employees; serving 10,000 special education students as well as 5,000 students per year in talents unlimited; providing adult education at no cost to over 4,500 adults per year; continuing to alleviate asbestos problems, providing bus transportation to 12% of all students; coordinating comprehensive food services.

The brochure also highlighted the emphasis placed on instruction which included system wide curriculum guides K-12, Chapter I services, and piloting the State Model of Project Adopt and initiating the Effective School Program. The brochure's third category entitled <u>Meets Special Needs</u>, described programs for at-risk students, alternative school, and a drop-out prevention program. It also emphasized the implementing of the Least Restrictive Environment Program for handicapped students, enrichment programs, the Adopt-A-School program with 100% of schools adopted by business as well as the development of a Teacher Center.

Unlike the first election, Mr. Hoffmeister had the publicized support of leading educators like Roy Mullins, Dink Adams, Bill Clabo, Fred Nideffer to name a few. Numerous educators and community leaders had publically stated that the first school year of the merged system had gone well despite lawsuits over pensions and continuing budget crises. Community leaders were quick to acknowledge that the quality of education had not suffered. Tommy Schumpert, Assistant, pointed out that the majority of students and teachers had not even noticed the change. He credited Mr. Hoffmeister and his staff with not trying to make big changes;

instead, the year was spent looking at both systems to try to make the transition as smooth as possible.

Mr. Hoffmeister followed his same political campaign that he had previously used. He insisted on keeping the campaign positive, no black eyes. "In the end one of us will be superintendent." He might have had a detailed, complex brochure, but when he spoke he kept it simple. When he discussed his leadership style he stated that he made over 300 school visits a year, he had quality people on his staff and he turned them lose to do their jobs. He stressed that he had never made a decision based on politics, that he worked cooperatively with both parties and cited the Republican-dominated school board as an example.

As the challenger, Wanda Moody had no choice but to attack and criticize the incumbent which is a difficult thing to do unless there are glaring failures on the part of your opponent. Miss Moody had a problem of zeroing in on issues that the voting public could latch onto. She cited examples of how the two systems had not totally merged, that there were still maintenance departments, some accounting mistakes in writing checks, problems over bus routes, not buying in bulk and so forth – but there was nothing to capitalize on.

Mr. Hoffmeister did respond to her platform and criticism in a very low key way. He pointed out that all school systems strive to do most of the things in Miss Moody's platform, and added that there were very few that his administration was not doing. He did point out that Wanda would have to clone herself to meet with the 90+ advisory committees she was advocating. He also pointed out that there were already either a PTA or PTO in most schools and booster clubs and advisory committees in the Chapter I schools.

His final assertion was that the merger and the school system was going well, and that you shouldn't change coaches in the middle of a winning season. Apparently, the voters agreed with him because on August 4, 1988, Earl Hoffmeister was reelected with an overwhelming majority; he carried 91 or the 96 precincts.

Campaigning is an integral and important part of any elected official's life and Earl was fortunate to have the support of wonderful campaign workers. The following photographs show some of these supporters who shared four victorious elections with Earl and, through their dedicated help, allowed him to retire undefeated.

Bill Padgett and wife are all smiles about election results.

Left to right, Margaret Clabo Pattison and JoAnne Hoffmeister at Earl's reelection campaign party, July 21, 1988.

EARL HOFFMEISTER KNOX COUNTY SCHOOLS SUPERINTENDENT

John R. McCloud and Mary Kerr, *Celebrating hand in hand*. Sketch of Earl in background was made by Fred Patterson.

Holding drink, tireless campaign worker, John Dobbs discusses events with Jack Cooper.

Left to right, Reed, Mary and Margaret Garrison; Paul Monger, co-campaign manager with campaign manager, Jean Payne. *In the background* is JoAnne and Earl Hoffmeister.

Most biographies like this one devote a lot of space to one leadership and management style of its' subjects. The two dissertations about Miss Doyle certainly contain large sections on the topics. Those dissertations and their descriptions are based on interviews with the key staff members which they select. The difference with this biography and the dissertations is that the descriptions in this one are "colored" by the fact that I worked for Miss Doyle for 13 years as a principal and supervisor and for Mr. Hoffmeister for 4 years as a supervisor. Also, there is no doctoral committee looking over my shoulder, so at this point I get the last word with no fear of rebuttal. I realize that the incidences I am going to cite are aimed at proving the point of view and opinions I have held for 25 years. Let the reader be warned.

Mr. Hoffmeister has been criticized by some as having no consistent management style: just bumbled along with various people actually really running the school system. I would be the first to admit that his leadership and management style was not taught in any course I ever had or found in any educational leadership text I ever paid too much for. It was pure Earl Hoffmeister.

Tommy Schumpert summed it up well when he said, "With Earl, what you see is what you get," and the people who worked for him trusted him for that reason. During recent interviews with secretarial staff that worked for both Miss Doyle and Mr. Hoffmeister, a few admitted to being afraid of Miss Doyle. I could confirm that. When she sent for you, you never knew if you were going to be chewed out or given a bag of walnuts she had picked up at the farm the previous night. I'm sure that a few people must have been reprimanded by Mr. Hoffmeister through the years, but I don't know anyone who felt intimidated.

Tommy Schumpert also stressed that Mr. Hoffmeister simply allowed everyone at every level to get on with what they did best. But he was nobody's fool. He often said that he didn't try to be smart; the Bible itself did not say much about smart people, but it did say a lot about being wise and that was what he tried to be. One good example of that was certainly not found in any management course.

A beginning teacher in one of the schools in West Knoxville became so discouraged that she spoke to a supervisor about her inability to do anything to please the principal. The supervisor tried to help the teacher, but to no avail. Finally, the supervisor mentioned it to Mr. Hoffmeister. He sent the teacher word by the supervisor that he would be visiting the school the next week and that when he came into her room she was to give him a big hug. True to his word, Mr. Hoffmeister did visit the school and he and the principal went from room to room. Mr. Hoffmeister had no idea of which teacher it was and entered each room wondering if this would be the one. Finally, to the amazement of the principal and the relief of Mr. Hoffmeister, a young teacher came up and threw her arms around him. Mr. Hoffmeister asked her how she was getting along and made his usual contacts with the students. That ended the teacher's problems and she really blossomed. Her evaluation was high enough from the principal for her to be chosen best teacher of the school the following year. Management style? Pure Hoffmeister.

Another problem was brought to Mr. Hoffmeister's attention when a teacher's brother telephoned a supervisor from out of state. The brother reported that his sister had been forced to pay over $450 because a piece was missing from a Science kit which the teacher had used. The teacher had written a check believing that she had no choice. The brother did not believe the action on the part of the principal who had made the demand was fair. Fortunately, the check was still in the business office. Mr. Hoffmeister marked it void and put it in his desk. The supervisor was to tell the teacher that the check would never clear her bank account. No fuss, no confrontation and again pure Hoffmeister who settled a problem without creating another one.

Mr. Hoffmeister established ideas of leadership early in his days in Central Office. An organizational chart had been drawn up following various power struggles to enlarge areas of supervision. Mr. Hoffmeister listened to everyone who had any comments about it. At the staff meeting to discuss the final draft, Mr. Hoffmeister turned the chart upside down – showing his position at the bottom of the organization. The people at the bottom, including himself, were low on the totem poll. They were there to support the teachers (now at the top) who actually did the work.

Hoffmeister also had his own style of handling community members who were dissatisfied. At that time, the parents in the Farragut area were very vocal with their demands for more and better facilities. Hoffmeister did not try to lessen their demands. Instead, he got a school bus and invited the most vocal parents to take a tour of schools in the East end of the county. They were appalled by the buildings and lack of facilities of schools like Skaggston, Mascot and John Sevier. At the end of the tour, they told him to take care of those schools first.

In a dispute involving a discipline issue at an elementary school, a parent was just insistent that the principal and the teacher were in the wrong in the statements concerning his son's behavior. The supervisor tried to resolve it without success. She finally told the parent the only thing left to do was for the parent to talk to the superintendent. An appointment was made and the irate father recounted the principal and the teacher's refusal to accept the boy's story. The parent ended with the declaration that his son did not lie.

Mr. Hoffmeister waited and listened carefully to every word the man had to say. At the end of it, Mr. Hoffmeister told him that he was really a lucky man if he could say that. Mr. Hoffmeister went on to say that every child he had would lie if anyone told anything that would get them in trouble. He then recounted a couple of incidences and said they finally found out that the truth was going to come out sooner or later and they did better. He ended with a chuckle that these days he believed most of all they said. The man was disarmed and said maybe he would just let it go this time and he and Hoffmeister went on with some other stories of when they were boys.

Mr. Hoffmeister often used the fact that he was held back in first grade to reassure people who came in to protect their children being held back. He said it seemed to be good for him. He could usually find a way around confrontation. His years as assistant principal responsible for discipline and as a coach were proof of his success with working with students as well as their parents.

There was also something unusual in Mr. Hoffmeister's office that must have had an effect on everyone sitting at the desk talking with him. This was a large painting of Jesus Christ listening intently to a man in a suit. If anyone ever objected to the portrait I never heard it, and Mr. Hoffmeister never had an objection. It certainly must have an effect on folks who came in angry and probably discouraged "colorful language." If you can imagine facing Mr. Hoffmeister seated at his desk with this portrait behind you, you can imagine the effect. Mr. Hoffmeister himself was an exceptional man – did not smoke or drink or use any kind of profanity. And yet he came across as a man's man. When someone asked when or what decided him not to smoke or drink or use profanity, he pointed out he started as a coach and couldn't ask his students to behave differently from himself.

Mr. Hoffmeister's leadership style also could be seen in the selection of the top staff in Central Office that he chose to be his "right arms" – Tommy Schumpert and Sarah Simpson. Both are still remembered for their integrity, their dedication and hard work, and they were approachable. One of their coworkers characterized them as having "smooth edges" and added that they must have been ambitious but that they concealed it well. In other words, he chose people that reflected his own values.

There were people that Mr. Hoffmeister disliked: in interviewing Tommy Schumpert for this biography we talked about the few people who made that list – you could count them on one hand. Their common denominator was the way they treated other people. He particularly disliked seeing educators trying to act superior because they had earned advanced degrees.

Tommy pointed out that the foundation of Earl's leadership and personality was that he treated everyone the same; that he truly was not a respecter of a person's position. It did not matter if you were

Tommy Schumpert.

President Reagan or the lowest paid maintenance worker, you received exactly the same friendly unpretentious attention. I doubt that Earl ever failed to talk to the custodial staff and the ladies in the kitchen at any school he ever visited. And he always took time to include students as he visited classes.

The reciprocal was also true. This spontaneous friendliness made Earl well liked by almost everyone he encountered. Even most of those, from all walks of life, who disagreed with some of his ideas or actions, still liked him. Certainly, this trait was important for a non-political person who depended on votes to win and hold a political position.

Two of his earliest supporters were Reverend J. Bazzel Mull and his wife Elizabeth—better known as Preacher and Lady or Miss Mull. For decades, they were legends on Knoxville radio and television. Preacher Mull was blinded as a baby and depended on Elizabeth, his constant companion, to be his eyes to the outside world. Earl felt his biography would not be complete without a photograph of them.

Preacher Mull and his wife Elizabeth (Lady Mull).

Chapter 6
Accomplishments and Honors

When Mr. Hoffmeister looks back at his accomplishments, he always begins with his determination to finish college without his parents having to foot the bill, although his parents were financially able and willing to cover his expenses. Earl takes great pride in telling how he accomplished that goal. He was awarded eight scholarships and worked numerous jobs in a cotton mill, as a mechanic and other menial jobs.

Like many of his generation, Earl also is proud that he was the first in his family to finish high school and then to graduate from college. Earl also accomplished a goal of being what many young men dream of being – "Saturday's Hero." Earl was an outstanding athlete from the time he entered Young High School. Earl played both basketball and football at Young High School, and he was Captain of both the basketball team and the football team! Both of the teams had outstanding records, in the basketball season of 1943-1944. The Yellow Jackets football team won 9 games, lost 2. In 1944-45, only three boys from the last

Earl in his football uniform. Captain of Young High Football Team - All East Tennessee Team.

year's first string were back; the others had gone into the military. The members who returned were Earl Hoffmeister, Roy Stokes and Willard Cheatam. The team won four games, tied two and lost four. But Earl was chosen to the 1944 *News-Sentinel* "All East Tennessee Team."

Earl also received the honor of being Mr. Young High as a Senior. He noted that every time he thinks of having the photograph made, he remembers he had to borrow Mr. Duff's jacket and pointed out that it was obvious in the photograph that the sleeves were too short.

Earl's last coaching years were at Powell High School when he was hired to replace his old friend, John Clabo, who went to Young High. He won Coach of the Year twice in four seasons. He coached basketball, just one year at Powell and won the district. Earl certainly achieved a lot in athletics. But he also stated in an interview with Marvin West, a Sports Writer for the *Knoxville News-Sentinel* that in addition to wanting to win games, his real objective in being a coach was to give back to sports what sports had given to him. His main reason for coaching was to help young people – that applied to him as a coach, a teacher, an assistant principal and later as a superintendent. If Earl had finished his career as assistant principal at Central High, he certainly would have been counted a success. His old principal, Dan Boring, described him as a good teacher who was well liked and known as being fair and that these characteristics carried over into his time as assistant principal. Former students and fellow teachers also used the same phrases, i.e., he was always fair and that he was well liked. In one episode at Central High School, Earl suspended a boy and was called into the Central Office. The rumor circulated that the superintendent was going to fire him if he would not back down. Everyone knew that Earl would not back down. The students at Central had secretly decided to walk out if it happened. But on advice from some of the Central Office staff, the superintendent "let him off with a warning" and the boy stayed suspended. When Earl and Mr. Boring, who had supported Earl's actions got back, they were amazed at what the students planned to do.

In 1992, when Earl completed his four terms as superintendent, he was finishing 40 years in education. In an interview with Betsy Koufman in the *Knoxville News-Sentinel*, Earl reminisced over his long and colorful career. He was leaving behind being superintendent of one of the largest public school systems in Tennessee (50,000 plus students) following the 1987 merger of the Knoxville and Knox County Systems. One of the first things he mentioned that he was proud of was a building program that has essentially doubled the number of schools in the system.

When Mr. Hoffmeister became Superintendent of Knox County in September 1976, some of the buildings were in a very poor condition. Among the ones in dire need of replacement were John Sevier, Mascot, and Skaggston in East Knox County; Hardin Valley, Heiskell and Green Hill in the West. These schools were beyond repair or renovation. Many others could be lined up for closure – White, High Bluff and Halls Elementary. Many of the other schools were also in critical need of repairs. The asbestos removal problem had just reared its ugly head. The lack of air conditioning demanded action and the maintenance problems were complicated by a series of fires and population explosions in other areas.

When Mr. Hoffmeister announced his candidacy in 1988 after having completed three terms, he could claim he had built, renovated and expanded 17 schools. He could also cite the current renovation of Vine Middle, Powell Elementary and Blue Grass was underway. On the drawing board were plans for the new Farragut Primary and a new construction project at West Hills Elementary.

Coming from a construction background, Mr. Hoffmeister took careful interest from the architects plans to the signing off and door opening of each school. Another demand for building and renovation of schools was that they had to be accessible to the handicapped. As Tommy Schumpert pointed out Earl wanted all the buildings to be sound and functional.

Mr. Hoffmeister was keenly interested in improving educational opportunities for all. He took particular pride in alternative learning programs such as the Center School where high school dropouts could return to earn credits to secure their standard diploma. He was also very supportive of Adult Education classes, where adults could attend to prepare for their G.E.D. as well as the Evening High School classes that offered a more traditional approach to completing high school.

One of the programs that was dear to Mr. Hoffmeister's heart was the Fort Sanders Educational Developmental Center where severely handicapped students were taught. Hanging in Mr. Hoffmeister's office was a picture of a laughing girl with

Earl and Peggy Dison, Homebound Student.

short dark hair and a sweet smile. She was a handicapped child who had died several years before. Earl confided that she was one of his favorite persons who couldn't move anything except her head. She represented all the students who had disabilities and yet remained smiling with whatever she could achieve. Mr. Hofmeister called her "Sugarfoot." He also kept a photograph of a young man in a wheelchair named Larry who was the first person to whom Mr. Hoffmeister issued a diploma.

Mr. Hoffmeister also listed high ACT scores that "mean our kids can go anywhere in the nation and do well." To many people's surprise who saw him as a coach first, Mr. Hoffmeister truly put instruction first. He strongly supported higher salaries for teachers, and said over and over again it was his and the rest of Central Office staff members' first responsibility to support the teachers who did the work. Tommy Schumpert stressed that Mr. Hoffmeister always backed the academics and had a great respect for Central Office Instructional Supervisors. Two of his closest advisors were Beecher Clapp and Sarah Simpson whom he viewed as

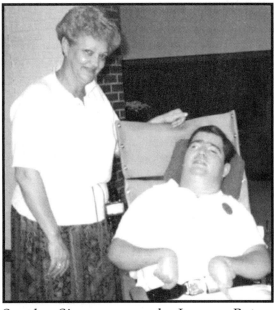

Sarah Simpson and Larry Bates, Homebound Student.

the top people in the state in the area of instruction and curriculum. He saw the Traveling Reading and Math Teachers as critical to student instructional improvement.

In his final interviews before retiring he also listed among the things he was proudest of was a successful program to fight drug and alcohol abuse. Mr. Hoffmeister saw these addictions as interfering in students learning. In the same manner he supported the Alternative Schools and classes that would enable students who had been expelled to continue their education.

Certainly, one of his major challenges and major successful accomplishments was the merger of Knoxville City and Knox County Schools. Despite lawsuits and disputed pension rights and continuing budget crisis, most educators agreed that the merger went well. Students and teachers hardly noticed the change because of the courteous approach the superintendent and his staff took. The merger resulted in a school system involving 92 schools, and approximately 50,000 students and 5000 professional staff. And, Mr. Hoffmeister again found himself starting with schools in dire need of maintenance and repair as well as a new set of problems including integration or desegregation issues that had not been resolved.

Hoffmeister reflected over the merging of the two systems and stated that over the years he wondered if it would not have been better if Knoxville City Schools had been allowed to continue as an independent system with both systems funded by Knox County Commission and one School Board. It's a thought provoking idea which would have kept the systems smaller and more manageable. It would have prevented some problems and, on the other hand, created others.

Mr. Hoffmeister was keenly interested and supportive of supplementary programs that advanced reading. The one that was in place when he took office in 1976 was Reading Is Fundamental that was in all the Knox County Schools – elementary, middle and high schools. Mr. Hoffmeister thoroughly enjoyed taking part in RIF days at various schools. At the time of his election through 1980, the author was the Director of RIF. Anytime Mr. Hoffmeister was out of the office and off his daily schedule, I would receive a phone call asking which schools were having RIF that day. One story that Earl loves to retell was his first visit to Skaggston Elementary where he had gone to meet the staff and to look over the condition of the building. When he arrived, Sue Boyer and others were chasing a pig down the hall. It was RIF day and one of the classes was washing the pig in buttermilk (*Charlotte's Web*) when the pig escaped! Later Sue would become the RIF Director and as Elementary Supervisor . . . and had to hear that story every time Earl had an opportunity to tell it.

Earl's list of achievements over his 16 years is impressive. The list includes the Adopt-A-School program that included all the schools, remedial school programs at 6 elementary, 8 middle and 2 high schools, expanding traveling specialists serving the system in music, science, mathematics, talented and gifted and computer education programs.

One of Mr. Hoffmeister's outstanding achievements if not the most notable has been his ability to gain and keep the loyalty of the people that he worked with. This dates back to his high school and college days and carries on through his 40 years in education and beyond. But it was especially evident in his beginning days in the superintendency. He walked into a Central Office, knowing practically no one, having defeated their superintendent, facing "Miss Doyle's staff" and winning them over in such an unobtrusive way that they became his staff. He began by asking Faye Cox, who had been Miss Doyle's secretary for several years to remain as his secretary, and she did until Mr. Hoffmeister retired. Dick Yoakley summed it up by saying that Mr. Hoffmeister was a leader who demonstrated compassion and believed that the very best in people emerges when their leader conveys belief and confidence in them. Tommy Schumpert said that Mr. Hoffmeister won that loyalty by just being what he was, treating everyone from President Reagan to the lowest paid food service worker just the same – and standing aside and allowing people to do what they did best.

A book of notes put together when Earl retired <u>echoed</u> the same sentiments. The same phrases - fairness, friendliness, humor, always listened, approachable, are mentioned over and over again. A humorous tribute called the <u>Good Ole Boy's Manual</u> which was dedicated to Knox County's favorite "Good Ole Boy" stressed the same characteristics that endeared Mr. Hoffmeister to the people of Knox County.

Highlights in Mr. Hoffmeister's tenure as Superintendent included visits of two U.S. Presidents – a first for Knox County Schools. In June of 1983, President Ronald Reagan made an afternoon visit to Farragut High School. His main purpose was to learn more about Governor Lamar Alexander's Master Teacher plan and to discuss incentive pay with the teachers at the luncheon. Thirty-two people attended the luncheon; there were 28 teachers including 5 from the Knoxville City Schools.

Following the luncheon, there was a panel discussion with school leaders in the auditorium in front of an audience that included 55 legislators, members of the interim commission, State Board of Education members and the National Principal of the Year, Emiral A. Crosby and the National Teacher of the Year, Jay Summer. Governor

Alexander led the panel discussion made up of legislators and members of the State Interim Commission.

But in many ways, it was President Reagan's visit to Shirley Mynatt's English Class where he repeated his convictions during a question and answer session. He also fielded a half a dozen other questions from students, including prayer in schools. He stated that he differed with the Supreme Court to take prayer out of schools. President Reagan also quoted part of *Macbeth* which the class was studying.

Mr. Hoffmeister said he was honored that President Reagan chose to visit Farragut High and Knox County Schools

Earl Hoffmeister and President Ronald Reagan, with Jim Bellamy, Principal of Farragut.

EARL HOFFMEISTER KNOX COUNTY SCHOOLS SUPERINTENDENT

out of the many schools throughout the nation. Hoffmeister, too, relished the President's remark that he made calling Farragut High School and Knox County School System as a "shining example of pubic education at its best . . .what better place for a President to take a few lessons for the country on quality education." Mr. Hoffmeister proudly displays a portrait of himself and President Reagan and a letter on his wall.

The second president, who was then Vice President, to visit a Knox County School was George H. Bush. Vice President Bush came for quite a different reason than President Reagan; it was in January 1988 before the election and Vice President Bush was on the campaign trail. Vice President Bush

Earl Hoffmeister and Vice President George H. Bush, with Rex Stooksbury.

met with his supporters as well as local officials which included Mr. Hoffmeister at Central High School. He had been met at the airport by Mayor Victor Ashe and his wife. Mayor

Ashe had gone to Yale with the Vice President's son, George Bush, Jr.; and several years later would be appointed Ambassador to Poland when George Bush, Jr. became President.

Earl Hoffmeister not only met Presidents and other high officials during his tenure as Superintendent, he received numerous honors. For example, in his last term he was named Outstanding Superintendent of the Year by the Tennessee Congress of Parents and Teachers. Council President, Diane Dozier, said in a prepared news release that Hoffmeister deserved the recognition for "his dedication to providing the best education to every child and for his genuine love and concern for children and youth during his 11 years as Superintendent and his 40 years in education."

In his study at home he has a wall of Certificates of Appreciation from Leadership America, United Way, Partners in Education to name a few. Trying to determine if there were others, I asked him were there any more. He smiled and said, "I ran out of wall." There are also autographed photos of Mr. Hoffmeister with President Reagan and Lamar Alexander along with a framed letter from President Reagan expressing his appreciation. Another photograph shows him with George H. Bush, who was then Vice President. Another photograph pictures him with Dolly Parton. All of these are reminders of highlights during his tenure as Superintendent.

A very memorable highlight following his retirement was his traveling with the Tennessee Children's Dance Ensemble Performing Tour to the Republic of China-Taiwan in October 1993.

This tour was under the sponsorship of the Pacific Cultural Foundation. On the trip were 19 dancers, 11-16 years of age, under the directorship of Dr. Dorothy Floyd and associate director Irene Lynn and the crew that makes up the

EARL HOFFMEISTER KNOX COUNTY SCHOOLS SUPERINTENDENT

Tennessee Children's Dance ensemble. Mr. Hoffmeister accompanied them as a chaperone and, as they were all officially designed – an Ambassador from Knoxville and Tennessee.

The tour included nine days of performances and demanding schedules of rehearsals, performances, meeting audiences and dignitaries. But it also included 5-Star hotels, seven course dinners and two days in Taiwan to experience the art, culture and religion. A highlight for Mr. Hoffmeister and the dancers was a special tour of the Palace Museum in Talpai.

Earl in Taiwan.

Another overseas trip that Earl enjoyed was a Safari to Africa sponsored by the Knoxville Zoo. The safari involved riding in an open Landrover to view the immense countryside of Kenya and Tanzania as well as seemingly endless kinds of elephants, buffaloes and numerous kinds of antelopes.

BENNA F. J. VAN VUUREN

Like most first time visitors to Kenya and Tanzania the immensity of the landscape was overwhelming – seeming to reach beyond forever. Few people, including Earl, ever forget the Sergatti Plains and the majesty of Mt. Kilimanjaro, Africa's tallest mountain, rising high above clouds in Tanzania.

The abundance and variety of wild life that one can see in these countries are familiar to viewers of wild life programs on television, but to see them in real life and up close is an entirely different experience. Experienced guides on the safari are pointing out and explaining the wild life and their habitat from the smallest insects to the majestic birds – from the small mammals to the largest. Mr. Hoffmester appreciated all of this as well as his first opportunity to see and talk to tribal people. Having lived in South Africa for 12 years and having been on safaris I could appreciate and see Kenya and Tanzania through Earl's eyes and share his puzzlement at the Kikuyers as well as the guides having trouble understanding him.

Earl on Safari.

Asking him about "roughing it" on safari brought a big smile. Excellent sleeping tents, gourmet meals, endless service is all part and parcel of "being on safari" in Africa. Earl thoroughly enjoyed the music, singing and dancing that the Africans provided as well as the beautiful crafts that were for sale.

One of the highlights of Mr. Hoffmeister's superintendency – and certainly a notable achievement – occurred in 1987. Dwight Kessel, Knox County Executive, telephoned him while he was on a short holiday at Myrtle Beach, North Carolina. Mr. Kessel told him about the possibility of securing $90 million to establish a corporation that could buy loans from student loan lenders to expand access to higher education to students.

The Volunteer State Student Funding Corporation was chartered in December 1987 because of Mr. Hoffmeister's and Mr. Kessel's effort and employed Tony Hollin as Executive Director and Sheila Walker as Executive Assistant.

Volunteer State Student Funding Corporation (VSSFC) evolved from a single purpose loan secondary market to a vertically integrated educational funding and servicing corporation. VSSFC began to loan directly to students in 1990 and to service loans in 1993. In 1996, the company separated to their relative business function; VSSFC was renamed Educational Funding of the South, Inc. (Edsouth) and the servicing corporation became EdFinancial Services. Edsouth became the largest and fastest growing secondary market in the South with loan holdings and commitments of over $4 billion. EdFinancial now provides services to 15 of the top 100 student lenders, employs 450 people and remains located in the Knoxville area.

The last company to evolve was Edamerica which loans money directly to students and is the second largest student loan lender that is not a bank; it is forecast to assist students with educational funding in the amount of $13 billion in 2006.

Equally impressive, if not more so, are the four public purpose programs. For the past four years, the companies have donated $12 million to assist students that showed interest in community services with scholarships. By August 2006, 600 students were participating. The Student Outreach Programs provide four counselors that travel the state spreading the word that a college degree is attainable. Edamerica has also provided the funding for a career assessment test. Last, but not least, Edamerica provide Ecampustours.com to provide visual tours of over 1,400 college campuses.

To the author, one of the most impressive things I learned about this highlight is that Tony Hollin who began as Executive Director in 1988 is now the Chairman and CEO of EdSouth/Edamerica and almost 20 years later remains enthusiastic not only about past achievements, but also about future possibilities.

It was Mr. Hollin who provided all the information included. It is also noteworthy that he credited Mr. Hoffmeister and the other original board members as having the vision and commitment and thus making all these programs happen.

Mr. Hoffmeister and Mr. Hollin share the experience of being the first members of their families to graduate from college. Both of them completed their degrees before the days of so many opportunities for financial funding. Both believe strongly in what Mr. Hollin stated so concisely, "Every student deserves that opportunity to be what he can be."

That belief seems to underwrite Earl Hoffmeister's accomplishments and achievements. It is easy to see in his own life as well as in his professional life. You also see it in the lives of people he has chosen for leadership roles like Tony Hollin. Earl's first choice for a leadership role in Central Office – Tommy Schumpert – is also very involved in the Edscholar

EARL HOFFMEISTER KNOX COUNTY SCHOOLS SUPERINTENDENT

Program of EdSouth/Edamerica. According to Earl, he just goes around giving away scholarships. But Google identifies him as the Program Director.

Chapter 7
Conclusions

Long after most people have forgotten just how long Mr. Hoffmeister served as Superintendent and exactly what problems, programs and changes occurred, his humor and non-traditional management style will be remembered. What other superintendent could you find that would take his tractor and remove snow from a school so the system could re-open? What other superintendent do you know that was willing to mortgage his house to fund textbooks for the schools?

This was the superintendent known for being frugal. A favorite story that made the rounds was about an incident that happened at McDonald's. Mr. Hoffmeister who had been working on a construction site, went in at lunchtime for a quick snack. In addition to ordering a Big Mac, fries and a drink, he also ordered two apple pies for $1, thinking he could save one of them for later. But he inadvertently threw away one when he emptied his tray in the trash container. Earl was not about to lose his apple pie.

While searching through the garbage, he felt a tap on the shoulder. When he turned around, there stood a woman with a dollar in her hand. She told him he didn't have to search the garbage for lunch. Here was a dollar to buy himself some lunch. Earl thanked her, took the dollar, picked up his apple pie which he had already located and left. Later he commented that he couldn't have bought much of a lunch for a dollar.

Faye Cox, who had been secretary to Miss Doyle and served as Mr. Hoffmeister's secretary for 16 years, makes no secret that her years with Mr. Hoffmeister were the most rewarding years of her career. Faye recounts various instances of Mr. Hoffmeister being very frugal with the County funds as well as his own. He regularly gave her money to purchase envelopes and stamps for his personal use. He did not attend the National Superintendent's Conferences because of the expense. But she recounted numerous times that he helped students who needed financial support in order to further their education. He was careful not to reveal his financial help. He personally paid tuition for a former student to attend nurses training. Another example which Faye cited was his assistance to a former student who had social and emotional problems. Not only did he counsel her, he even paid her rent and helped her find employment.

But if Faye was quick to tell of his generosity, she was also quick to remember a story that "beat Mr. Hoffmeister back home." He went on a company paid trip to California sponsored by Apple Computer Company when the personal computers first came out. Mr. Hoffmeister evidently was quite impressed by all he saw and heard. He told one of the presenters that as soon as we got indoor plumbing in all the schools, he was going to buy one of them. Whereupon the company gave him one to bring back. Central Office Staff was never sure whether the Apple folks realized it was said in jest.

Faye and others in Central Office had a laugh or two at Hoffmeister's expense about his overconfidence of solving a dispute involving the selection of cheerleaders at Farragut. He left Central Office confident that one short trip would do it. But it didn't and the dispute continued, involving lawyers and the School Board. At the next staff meeting Faye, Doris Jane Large and Barbara Webster popped in and started a cheer. "Two bits, four bits, six bits a dollar, all for Central Office stand up and holler."

This event shocked the staff so much that J. B. Bolin remarked that he thought Helen Reagan was having a heart attack. Faye was mortified at what they had done and expected to be fired, or at least disciplined. Instead, Mr. Hoffmeister just grinned and the three began to expect a retaliation. At the next staff meeting, the three were sent for and a poster of 3 little pigs dressed up as cheerleaders was presented to them. Fred Nidiffer had drawn the poster. The three "little pigs" were temporarily stunned, but recovered quickly and started singing "Lay's Three Little Pigs" jingle.

There are numerous other Hoffmeister stories out there, and I hope that this biography might encourage other people to write their favorite stories down and add them to the memories being collected by the Knox County Museum of Educational History, for it is the stories and anecdotes that turn history and people into a great collective history of any time.

I had admired Mr. Hoffmeister long before I began writing his biography, but that admiration grew as I spent more and more time interviewing him, his family and his friends – and reading various interviews and commentaries. Reflecting on my first impression of Mr. Hoffmeister when he walked into Central Office in 1976, I remembered wondering if he could be a "White Knight" - a man who could be trusted with Knox County Schools. Sixteen years in office may not have resulted in him being knighted, but those years proved that he could be trusted with Knox County Schools.

Folks would probably hoot at Mr. Hoffmeister being referred to as a "white knight" or having the characteristics of what Tennesseans see as heroic marks. We are much more comfortable with referring to Earl as our favorite Good Ole Boy, but then we proceed to give Good Ole Boys the same characteristics that we give our folk heroes.

Label Earl Hoffmeister with whatever you feel comfortable with – but here is the man who is quietly religious – a man who doesn't smoke, drink or use profane language – a humble man who never claimed to be more or know more than he did. Ask his secretary about kindness – exasperating her at times of him not being "a little bit mean" to those who opposed him the most.

Hoffmeister was certainly a tough opponent on the football field. He showed the same courage and determination in every aspect of his life. He dared to run against one of the most powerful and popular politicians of the day – Mildred E. Doyle and had the faith to believe in himself to believe he could win, and he did. He recalled that walking into Central Office that first time was just as much a challenge. But walk in he did and with just being himself won the majority of that staffs loyalty and love. He would be remembered and spoken of as a kind man, a compassionate man who treated everyone the same.

Mr. Hoffmeister dared to step aside and let everyone do what they knew how to do. He was not threatened by excellence in others nor lack of experience in himself. There was no doubt in anyone's mind for any length of time as to who was Superintendent of Knox County Schools and that Knox County Schools were safe in his hands.

BENNA F. J. VAN VUUREN

References/Acknowledgments

Baker, Carol E., *Superintendent Mildred E. Doyle: Educational Leader, Politician, Woman.* (Ed. D. U.T. 1977)

McGarrh, Kellie. (Hanging Tough) *Mildred E. Doyle Superintendent.* (Ed D.U.T. 1955).

Newspaper clippings from *Knoxville News-Sentinel*

Personal Interviews

EARL HOFFMEISTER KNOX COUNTY SCHOOLS SUPERINTENDENT

Appendix I

1975 - 1976

KNOX COUNTY BOARD OF EDUCATION

Ed Litton	Chairman
Kathleen Benson	Vice Chairman
Kathryn Barnhill	Fred Musick
Fred Graves	Leola Parks
Paul E. Hodges	Tommie Walker
A. L. Lots	

KNOX COUNTY QUARTERLY COURT

Andrew J. Dix	Alfred B. Bell
Walter S. E. Hardy	James K. Dyer
Jesse V. Cawood	James E. Cole
Billy G. Tindell	Willard V. Yarbrough
John A. Cox, Jr.	Ernest C. Battershell
Bruce Rankin	Joe M. McMillan
John G. Adams	Frank C. Carpenter
Max Wolf	Robert C. Easley
Robert M. Hill	C. E. (Red) Pitner
Gene Brady	

ADMINISTRATIVE STAFF

Mildred E. Doyle	Superintendent
Mildred M. Patterson	Administrative Assistant, Personnel
Beecher E. Clapp	Director of Instruction

BENNA F. J. VAN VUUREN

ADMINISTRATIVE STAFF (Continued)

C. M. Daugherty	Business Manager
Archer Bardes	Adult Education
Sam Bratton	Research and Evaluation
Mary Carroll	School Psychologist
Bob Chambers	Science
Joseph Chandler	Personnel
Charleen DeRidder	Mathematics
Jane Doyle	Social Studies
Bob Goff	Supervisor of Middle Schools
Bruce Hinton	Vocational Education
Mary Jo Husk	Elementary Education
Katherine Johnson	Materials and Library Service
VaLera Lewis	Art
J. B. Lyle	Choral and Instrumental Music
Bill Neal	Special Education
Paul Nicely	Maintenance
Bill Orr	Census and Attendance
J. W. Phifer	Secondary Education
Helen Regan	Food Services
LaNoka Rhodes	Elementary Education
James Robinson	Federal Projects
Ruth Sams	Kindergarten
Willa Selvey	Elementary Education
Sarah Simpson	Language Arts
Carolyn Sullivan	Health, Physical Education, Driver Education
Virginia Underwood	Reading
Bennie D. vanVuuren	Title I Consultant
Earl Wood	Transportation
Richard Yoakley	Guidance and Psychological Services

EARL HOFFMEISTER KNOX COUNTY SCHOOLS SUPERINTENDENT

<u>1976 - 1977</u>

KNOX COUNTY BOARD OF EDUCATION

Ed Litton	Chairman
Kathleen Benson	Vice Chairman
Fred Graves	Fred Musick
Jerry Hixson	Leola Parks
Paul E. Hodges	Tommie Walker
A. L. Lots	

KNOX COUNTY QUARTERLY COURT

Charles (Pete) Drew	H. B. Jenkins, Jr.
Walter S. E. Hardy	Joseph H. Pennell
Jesse V. Cawood	Mary Lou Horner
Billy G. Tindell	Willard V. Yarbrough
William F. Schaad	Billy J. Walker
William E. Jones	Joe McMillan
Dee DeSelm	Robert C. Easley
Max Wolf	Olen Ford
Ted S. Lundy	John R. Mills
Robert M. Hill	

ADMINISTRATIVE STAFF

Earl Hoffmeister	Superintendent
Fred Bedelle	Administrative Assistant
Sam Bratton	Research and Evaluation
Mary Carroll	School Psychologist
Bob Chambers	Science

BENNA F. J. VAN VUUREN

ADMINISTRATIVE STAFF (Continued)

Joseph Chandler	Personnel
Beecher E. Clapp	Director of Instruction
Ruth Clapp	Kindergarten
Charleen DeRidder	Mathematics
Jane Doyle	Social Studies
Bob Goff	Supervisor of Middle Schools
Bruce Hinton	Director of Vocational Education
Lib Hotchkiss	Supervisor of Materials and Library Service
Mary Jo Husk	Elementary Education
VaLera Lewis	Art
J. B. Lyle	Choral and Instrumental Music
Bill Neal	Special Education
Paul Nicely	Maintenance
Bill Orr	Transportation
J. W. Phifer	Secondary Education
Helen Regan	Food Services
LaNoka Rhodes	Elementary Education
James Robinson	Federal Projects
Willa Selvey	Elementary Education
Sarah Simpson	Language Arts
Carolyn Sullivan	Health, Physical Education, Driver Education
Virginia Underwood	Reading
Bennie D. vanVuuren	Title I Consultant
Richard Yoakley	Guidance and Psychological Services

EARL HOFFMEISTER KNOX COUNTY SCHOOLS SUPERINTENDENT

1977 - 1978

KNOX COUNTY BOARD OF EDUCATION

A. L. Lotts	Chairman
Kathleen Benson	Vice Chairman
Fred Graves	Fred Musick
Jerry Hixson	Leola Parks
Paul E. Hodges	Tommie Walker
Ed Litton	

KNOX COUNTY QUARTERLY COURT

Charles (Pete) Drew	H. B. Jenkins, Jr.
Walter S. E. Hardy	Joseph H. Pennell
Jesse V. Cawood	Mary Lou Horner
Billy G. Tindell	Willard V. Yarbrough
William F. Schaad	Billy J. Walker
William E. Jones	Joe McMillan
Dee DeSelm	Robert C. Easley
Max Wolf	Olen Ford
Ted S. Lundy	John R. Mills
Robert M. Hill	

ADMINISTRATIVE STAFF

Earl Hoffmeister	Superintendent
Fred Bedelle	Administrative Assistant
Sam Bratton	Research and Evaluation
Mary Carroll	School Psychologist
Bob Chambers	Science

BENNA F. J. VAN VUUREN

ADMINISTRATIVE STAFF (Continued)

Joseph Chandler	Personnel
Beecher E. Clapp	Director of Instruction
Ruth Clapp	Kindergarten
Charleen DeRidder	Mathematics
Jane Doyle	Social Studies
Faye Gluck	Social Services
Bob Goff	Middle Schools
Bruce Hinton	Director of Vocational Education
Lib Hotchkiss	Materials and Library Service
Mary Jo Husk	Elementary Education
VaLera Lewis	Art
J. B. Lyle	Choral and Instrumental Music
Barbara Neal	Guidance
Bill Neal	Special Education
Bill Orr	Transportation
J. W. Phifer	Secondary Education
Helen Regan	Food Services
LaNoka Rhodes	Elementary Education
James Robinson	Federal Projects
Thomas Schumpert	Business Manager
Willa Selvey	Elementary Education
Sarah Simpson	Language Arts
Carolyn Sullivan	Health, Physical Education, Driver Education
L. E. Turner	Maintenance
Virginia Underwood	Reading
Bennie D. vanVuuren	Title I Consultant
Richard Yoakley	Guidance and Psychological Services

EARL HOFFMEISTER KNOX COUNTY SCHOOLS SUPERINTENDENT

1978 - 1979

KNOX COUNTY BOARD OF EDUCATION

V. A. Anderson	Chairman
Kathleen Benson	Vice Chairman
Daniel Cooper	A. O. Lotts
John Cox	Jack Nichols
Jerry Hixson	Tommie Walker
W. B. Housley	

KNOX COUNTY QUARTERLY COURT

Charles (Pete) Drew	H. B. Jenkins, Jr.
Walter S. E. Hardy	Joseph H. Pennell
Jesse V. Cawood	Mary Lou Horner
Billy G. Tindell	Willard V. Yarbrough
William F. Schaad	Billy J. Walker
William E. Jones	Joe McMillan
Dee DeSelm	Robert C. Easley
Max Wolfe	Olen Ford
Ted S. Lundy	John R. Mills
Robert M. Hill	

ADMINISTRATIVE STAFF

Earl Hoffmeister	Superintendent
Fred Bedelle, Jr.	Administrative Assistant
Sam Bratton	Research and Evaluation
Mary Carroll	School Psychologist

BENNA F. J. VAN VUUREN

ADMINISTRATIVE STAFF (Continued)

Bob Chambers	Science
Joseph Chandler	Personnel
Beecher E. Clapp	Director of Instruction
Ruth Clapp	Kindergarten
Charleen DeRidder	Mathematics
Jane Doyle	Social Studies
Bob Goff	Supervisor of Middle Schools
Bruce Hinton	Director of Vocational Education
Lib Hotchkiss	Supervisor of Materials and Library Service
Mary Jo Husk	Elementary Education
VaLera Lewis	Art
J. B. Lyle	Choral and Instrumental Music
Bill Neal	Special Education
Bill Orr	Transportation
J. W. Phifer	Secondary Education
Helen Regan	Food Services
LaNoka Rhodes	Elementary Education
James Robinson	Federal Projects
Tomas Schumpert	Business Manager
Willa Selvey	Elementary Education
Sarah Simpson	Language Arts
Carolyn Sullivan	Health, Physical Education, Driver Education
L. E. Turner	Maintenance
Virginia Underwood	Reading
Bennie D. vanVuuren	Title I Consultant
Richard Yoakley	Guidance and Psychological Services

EARL HOFFMEISTER KNOX COUNTY SCHOOLS SUPERINTENDENT

1979 - 1980

KNOX COUNTY BOARD OF EDUCATION

Anderson	Chairman
Kathleen Benson	Vice Chairman
Daniel Cooper	A. L. Lotts
John Cox	Jack Nichols
Jerry Hixson	Tommie Walker
W. B. Housley	

KNOX COUNTY QUARTERLY COURT

Charles (Pete) Drew	H. B. Jenkins, Jr.
Walter S. E. Hardy	Joseph H. Pennell
Jesse V. Cawood	Mary Lou Horner
Billy G. Tindell	Willard V. Yarbrough
William F. Schaad	Billy J. Walker
William E. Jones	Joe McMillan
Dee DeSelm	Robert C. Easley
Max Wolfe	Olen Ford
Ted S. Lundy	John R. Mills
Robert M. Hill	

ADMINISTRATIVE STAFF

Earl Hoffmeister	Superintendent
Fred Bedelle	Administrative Assistant
Moonyean Bell	Special Education
J. B. Bolin, Jr.	Adult Basic Education
Alfred B. Bell	Social Studies
Sam Bratton	Research and Evaluation

BENNA F. J. VAN VUUREN

ADMINISTRATIVE STAFF (Continued)

Mary Carroll	School Psychologist
Bob Chambers	Science
Joseph Chandler	Personnel
Beecher E. Clapp	Director of Instruction
Herbert Clement	Vocational Curriculum Specialist
Charleen DeRidder	Mathematics
Faye Gluck	Social Services
Bob Goff	Supervisor of Middle Schools
John Hays	Transportation
Bruce Hinton	Director of Vocational Education
Leolah Hodge	Guidance, Health
Lib Hotchkiss	Supervisor of Materials and Library Service
Ray Jones	Vocational Education
VaLera Lewis	Art
J. B. Lyle	Choral and Instrumental Music
Lawrence Major	Maintenance, Adult Vocational Education
Bill Orr	Transportation
J. W. Phifer	Secondary Education
Helen Regan	Food Services
LaNoka Rhodes	Elementary Education
James Robinson	Federal Projects
Anne Roney	Elementary Education
Thomas Schumpert	Business Manager
Willa Selvey	Elementary Education
Sarah Simpson	Language Arts
Carolyn Sullivan	Health, Physical Education, Driver Education
L.E. Turner	Maintenance
Virginia Underwood	Reading
Bennie D. van Vuuren	Title I Consultant
Richard Yoakley	Guidance and Psychological Services

EARL HOFFMEISTER KNOX COUNTY SCHOOLS SUPERINTENDENT

1980 - 1981

KNOX COUNTY BOARD OF EDUCATION

Vernon Anderson	Chairman
Mickey Jeffries	Vice Chairman
John Cox	W. B. Housley
Kathleen Benson	Wayne S. Cannon
A. L. Lotts	Jack Nichols
Daniel Cooper	

KNOX COUNTY COMMISSIONERS

Charles (Pete) Drew	Jim Harbin
Walter S. E. Hardy	Ralph Teague
Jesse V. Cawood	Mary Lou Horner
Billy G. Tindell	William Pavlis
Rex Norman	Joe McMillan
Bruce Rankin	Billy J. Walker
Dee DeSelm	Olen Ford
Max Wolf	Tommy Lowe
Hassel Evans	John R. Mills
Frank Leuthoid	

ADMINISTRATIVE STAFF

Earl Hoffmeister	Superintendent
Fred Bedelle	Administrative Assistant
Alfred Bell	Social Studies
Moonyean Bell	Special Services
Anna Bellamy	Vocational Educational Resource

BENNA F. J. VAN VUUREN

ADMINISTRATIVE STAFF (Continued)

J. B. Bolin, Jr.	Adult Basic Education
Susan Bolt	Special Education Resource
Sue Boyer	Parent Involvement Coordinator
Sam Bratton	Research and Education
Dale Brown	Coordinator of Drive Ed Simulators
Pat Brown	Music Consultant
Mary Carroll	School Psychologist
Bob Chambers	Science
Joseph Chandler	Personnel
Beecher E. Clapp	Director of Instruction
Jo Allen Cook	Program Development & Evaluation
Charleen DeRidder	Mathematics
Marie Freeman	Vocational Education Resource
Faye Gluck	Social Services
Bob Goff	Supervisor of Middle Schools
John Hays	Transportation
Bruce Hinton	Director of Vocational Education
Leulah Hodge	Guidance, Heath
Lib Hotchkiss	Materials and Library Service
Ray Jones	Vocational Education
VaLera Lewis	Art
J. B. Lyle	Choral and Instrumental Music
Lawrence Major	Maintenance, Adult Voc. Ed.
Bill Orr	Attendance and Adm. Service
J. W. Phifer	Secondary Education
Helen Regan	Food Services
LaNoka Rhodes	Elementary Education
James Robinson	Federal Projects
Anne Roney	Elementary Education
Thomas Schumpert	Business Manager
Willa Selvey	Elementary Education

EARL HOFFMEISTER KNOX COUNTY SCHOOLS SUPERINTENDENT

ADMINISTRATIVE STAFF (Continued)

Sarah Simpson	Language Arts
Sally Sinclair	Title I Language Development
Carolyn Sullivan	Health, Physical Education
L. E. Turner	Maintenance
Virginia Underwood	Reading
Robert Werner	VAP Job Placeament
Richard Yoakley	Guidance and Psychological Services

1981 - 1982

KNOX COUNTY BOARD OF EDUCATION

Vernon Anderson	Chairman
Mickey JeffriesVice	Chairman

John Cox	W. B. Housley
Kathleen Benson	Wayne Cannon
A. L. Lotts	Jack Nichols
Daniel Cooper	

KNOX COUNTY COMMISSIONERS

Charles (Pete) Drew	Jim Harbin
Walter S. E. Hardy	Ralph Teague
Jesse V. Cawood	Mary Lou Horner
Billy G. Tindell	William Pavlis
Rex Norman	Joe McMillan
Bruce Rankin	Billy J. Walker
Dee DeSelm	Olen Ford
Max Wolf	Tommy Lowe

BENNA F. J. VAN VUUREN

KNOX COUNTY COMMISSIONERS (Continued)

Hassel Evans					John R. Mills
Frank Leuthoid

ADMINISTRATIVE STAFF

Earl Hoffmeister	Superintendent
Fred Bedelle	Administrative Assistant
Alfred Bell	Social Studies
Moonyean Bell	Special Services
Anna Bellamy	Vocational Educational Resource
J. B. Bolin, Jr.	Adult Basic Education
Susan Bolt	Special Education Resource
Sue Boyer	Parent Involvement Coordinator
Jacque Bradford	Language Arts
Sam Bratton	Research and Education
Pat Brown	Music Consultant
Mary Carroll	School Psychologist
Bob Chambers	Science
Joseph Chandler	Personnel
Joe Allen Cook	Special Programs
Charleen DeRidder	Mathematics
Marie Freeman	Vocational Education Resource
Faye Gluck	Social Services
Bob Goff	Middle Schools
John Hays	Transportation
Bruce Hinton	Vocational Education
Leulah Hodge	Guidance, Heath
Lib Hotchkiss	Materials Center
Ray Jones	Vocational Education
VaLera Lewis	Art
J. B. Lyle	Music

EARL HOFFMEISTER KNOX COUNTY SCHOOLS SUPERINTENDENT

ADMINISTRATIVE STAFF (Continued)

Lawrence Major	Maintenance
Bill Orr	Attendance and Adm. Service
J. W. Phifer	Secondary Education
Helen Regan	Food Services
LaNoka Rhodes	Elementary Education
James Robinson	Federal Projects
Anne Roney	Elementary Education
Thomas Schumpert	Business Manager
Willa Selvey	Elementary Education
Sarah Simpson	Acting Director of Instruction
Sally Sinclair	Title I
Carolyn Sullivan	Health, Physical Education
Virginia Underwood Kitts	Reading
Robert Werner	VAP
Richard Yoakley	Pupil Personnel

BENNA F. J. VAN VUUREN

SCHOOL PRINCIPALS   1976-1977

HIGH SCHOOLS

Byington-Solway Vocational Center	H. B. Jenkins
Carter High	David Wetzel
Doyle High	Billy K. Nicely
Farragut High	James Bellamy
Gibbs High	Max Clendenen
Halls High	Roy Mullins
Karns High	Leland Lyon
Knox-Union Vocational	Leonard Shepherd
Powell High	Jim Monroe, Leolah Hodge

MIDDLE SCHOOLS

Carter Middle	Harry Whitt
Cedar Bluff Middle	George Perry
Farragut Middle	Dr. Don Rhodes
Doyle Middle	Joe Goodlin
Halls Middle	James Ivey
Karns Middle	Bill Thomas
Powell Middle	Ben Stewart

ELEMENTARY SCHOOLS

Adrian Burnett	James Prince
Ball Camp	Andrew Shockley
Blue Grass	Joe Stewart
Bonny Kate	Dr. Ann Roney
Brickey	John R. McCloud
Carter	Bill Huffaker
Cedar Bluff Intermediate	Joe Tate

EARL HOFFMEISTER KNOX COUNTY SCHOOLS SUPERINTENDENT

ELEMENTARY SCHOOLS (Continued)

Cedar Bluff Primary	Wayne Smith
Corryton	George R. Martin
Fairview	Gladys Everett
Farragut Intermediate	Robert Frazier
Farragut Primary	Muriel Chreist
Gap Creek	James C. King
Gibbs	James Thurman
Green Hill	A. L. Strom
Halls	Scott Haynes
Hardin Valley	Gladys Everett
Heiskell	A. L. Strom
High Bluff	Janet Cruze
John Sevier	James Ray Ross
Karns	Arthur Swaggerty
Mascot	Lee Vittetoe
Mount Olive	Robert Huff
New Hopewell	Mayford Galyon
Powell	Fred West
Ramsey	Bill Maynard
Ritta	J. C. Jones
Riverdale	Bill Maynard
Skaggston	Wanda Johnston
Sunnyview	Virginia Lewis
Vestal	Ben Burnette
White	Janet Cruze

BENNA F. J. VAN VUUREN

SCHOOL PRINCIPALS   1977-1978

HIGH SCHOOLS

Byington-Solway Vocational Center	H. B. Jenkins
Carter High	David Wetzel
Doyle High	Billy K. Nicely
Farragut High	James Bellamy
Gibbs High	Max Clendenen
Halls High	Roy Mullins
Karns High	Leland Lyon
Knox-Union Vocational	Leonard Shepherd
Powell High	Jim Monroe, Leolah Hodge

MIDDLE SCHOOLS

Carter Middle	Harry Whitt
Cedar Bluff Middle	George Perry
Farragut Middle	Dr. Don Rhodes
Doyle Middle	Dr. Alvin Scott
Halls Middle	James Ivey
Karns Middle	Bill Thomas
Powell Middle	Ben Stewart

ELEMENTARY SCHOOLS

Adrian Burnett	James Prince
Amherst Kindergarten	Janet Oakes
Ball Camp	Andrew Shockley
Blue Grass	Joe Stewart
Bonny Kate	Dr. Ann Roney
Brickey	John R. McCloud
Carter	Bill Huffaker

EARL HOFFMEISTER KNOX COUNTY SCHOOLS SUPERINTENDENT

ELEMENTARY SCHOOLS (Continued)

Cedar Bluff Intermediate	Joe Tate
Cedar Bluff Primary	Wayne Smith
Corryton	George R. Martin
Fairview	Fred Russell
Farragut Intermediate	Dr. Robert Frazier
Farragut Primary	Muriel Chreist
Gap Creek	James C. King
Gibbs	James Thurman
Green Hill	
Halls	Scott Haynes
Hardin Valley	James Watkins
Heiskell	James Ray Ross
High Bluff	Janet Cruze
John Sevier	Elnora Williams
Karns	Arthur Swaggerty
Mascot	Sandra Hamilton
Mount Olive	Robert Huff
New Hopewell	Mayford Galyon
Powell	Fred West
Ramsey	Judy Presnell
Ritta	J. C. Jones
Riverdale	Bill Maynard
Skaggston	Wanda Johnston
Sunnyview	Virginia Lewis
Vestal	Ben Burnette
White	Charles Cameron

BENNA F. J. VAN VUUREN

SCHOOL PRINCIPALS   1980-1981

HIGH SCHOOLS

Byington-Solway Vocational Center	H. B. Jenkins
Carter High	Bob Pollard
Doyle High	
Farragut High	James Bellamy
Gibbs High	Jerry Sharp
Halls High	Roy Mullins
Karns High	Leland Lyon
Knox-Union Vocational	Leonard Shepherd
Powell High	Allen Morgan

MIDDLE SCHOOLS

Carter Middle	Harry Whitt
Cedar Bluff	George Perry
Farragut Middle	Dr. Donald Rhodes
Doyle Middle	Dr. Alvin Scott
Halls Middle	James Ivey
Karns Middle	Jim Monroe
Powell Middle	Benton Stewart

ELEMENTARY SCHOOLS

Adrian Burnett	James Prince
Amherst Kindergarten	Janet Oakes
Ball Camp	Andrew Shockley
Blue Grass	Joe Stewart
Bonny Kate	Lewis P. Robinette
Brickey	John R. McCloud
Carter	Bill Huffaker

EARL HOFFMEISTER KNOX COUNTY SCHOOLS SUPERINTENDENT

ELEMENTARY SCHOOLS (Continued)

Cedar Bluff Intermediate	Fred Nidiffer
Cedar Bluff Primary	Wayne Smith
Corryton	George R. Martin
East Knox	David Wetzel
Fairview/Hardin Valley	Fred Russell
Farragut Intermediate	Robert Frazier
Farragut Primary	Muriel Chreist
Gap Creek	James C. King
Gibbs	James Thurman
Halls	
High Bluff	Janet Cruze
Karns	Arthur Swaggerty
Mount Olive	Robert Huff
New Hopewell	Mayford Galyon
Powell	Fred West
Ramsey	Judy Presnell
Ritta	J. C. Jones
Riverdale	Lee Vittetoe
Sunnyview	Bill Thomas
Vestal	Ben Burnette
Young	Tom Moorehead
White	Charles Cameron

BENNA F. J. VAN VUUREN

SCHOOL PRINCIPALS 1981-1982

HIGH SCHOOLS

Byington-Solway Vocational Center	H. B. Jenkins
Carter High	Bob Pollard
Doyle High	Dr. Sandra Quillen
Farragut High	James Bellamy
Gibbs High	Max Clendenen
Halls High	Roy Mullins
Karns High	R. T. Everette
Knox-Union Vocational	Leonard Shepherd
Powell High	Allen Morgan

MIDDLE SCHOOLS

Carter Middle	Bobby Gratz
Cedar Bluff Middle	George Perry
Farragut Middle	Dr. Don Rhodes
Doyle Middle	Dr. Alvin Scott
Halls Middle	James Ivey
Karns Middle	Jim Monroe
Powell Middle	Benton Stewart

ELEMENTARY SCHOOLS

Adrian Burnett	James Prince
Ball Camp	Andrew Shockley
Blue Grass	Joe Stewart
Bonny Kate	
Brickey	John R. McCloud
Carter	Bill Huffaker
Cedar Bluff Intermediate	Fred Nidiffer

EARL HOFFMEISTER KNOX COUNTY SCHOOLS SUPERINTENDENT

ELEMENTARY SCHOOLS (Continued)

Cedar Bluff Primary	Wayne Smith
Corryton	George R. Martin
Fairview	
Farragut Intermediate	Dr. Robert Frazier
Farragut Primary	Muriel Chreist
Gap Creek	James C. King
Gibbs	James Thurman
Green Hill	
Halls	Scott Hayes
Karns	Ben Burnette
Karns Intermediate	Fred Russell
Mascot	
Mount Olive	Robert Huff
New Hopewell	
Powell	
Ramsey	Janet Cruze
Ritta	J. W. Jones
Riverdale	Elvin Vittetoe
Sunnyview	Bill Thomas
Vestal	Leland Lyon
Young Center	Tom Moorehead

BENNA F. J. VAN VUUREN

SCHOOL PRINCIPALS   1986-1987

HIGH SCHOOLS

Byington-Solway Vocational Center	H. B. Jenkins
Carter High	Bob Pollard
Doyle High	Dr. Sandra Quellen
Farragut High	James Bellamy
Gibbs High	Jerry Sharp
Halls High	Roy Mullins
Karns High	R. T. Everette
North Knox Vocational Center	Leonard Shepherd
Powell High	Allen Morgan

MIDDLE SCHOOLS

Carter Middle	Sandra Hamilton
Cedar Bluff Middle	George Perry
Farragut Middle	Dr. Don Rhodes
Doyle Middle	Dr. Alvin Scott
Halls Middle	James Ivey
Karns Middle	Jim Monroe
Powell Middle	Benton Stewart

ELEMENTARY SCHOOLS

Adrian Burnett	James Prince
Ball Camp	Dr. Ray Ross
Blue Grass	Joe Stewart
Bonny Kate	L. Pat Robinette
Brickey	John R. McCloud
Carter	Bill Huffaker
Cedar Bluff Intermediate	Fred Nediffer

EARL HOFFMEISTER KNOX COUNTY SCHOOLS SUPERINTENDENT

ELEMENTARY SCHOOLS (Continued)

Cedar Bluff Primary	Wayne Smith
Copper Ridge	Andrw Shockley
Corryton	George R. Martin
East Knox	Judy Cupp
Farragut Intermediate	Dr. Robert Frazier
Farragut Primary	Muriel Chreist
Fort Sanders Development Center	Tom Moorehead
Gap Creek	Jan Cruze
Gibbs	James Thurman
Green Hill	
Halls	Scott Haynes
Karns Intermediate	Fred Russell
Karns Primary	Ben Burnett
Mount Olive	Robert Huff
New Hopewell	Mayford Galyon
Powell	Freda Eidson
Ritta	J. C. Jones
Riverdale	Bill Maynard
Skaggston	Wanda Johnston
Sunnyview	Virginia Lewis
Vestal	Ben Burnette
White	Janet Cruze

BENNA F. J. VAN VUUREN

SUPERINTENDENTS OF KNOX COUNTY SCHOOLS

1. M. C. Wilcott (1869 - 1873)
2. T. C. Karns (1873 - 1875)
3. H. M. Brothers (1875 - 1877)
4. H. G. Hamstead (1877 - 1879)
5. F. M. Smith (1879 - 1880)
6. William Carroll Gibbs (1881 - 1883)
7. John R. Shipe (1883 - 1885)
8. J.W. Taylor (1885 - 1889)
9. J. C. Ford (1889 - 1897)
10. D. P. Duggan (1897 - 1901)
11. Sam E. Hills (1901 - 1907)
12. E. R. Cates (1907 - 1910)
13. M. W. Wilson (1911 - 1917)
14. W. L. Stooksbury (1917- 1923)
15. W. M. Morris (1923 - 1934)
16. Leonard Brickey (1934- 1946)
17. Mildred E. Doyle (1946-1976)
18. Earl Hoffmeister (1976 - 1992)
19. Allan Morgan (1992 - 1998)
20. Roy Mullins (1998 - 1999)
21. Charles Lindsey (1999 - Present)